Metaphors and Symbols

Metaphors and Symbols

Forays into Language

Roland Bartel
University of Oregon

National Council of Teachers of English
1111 Kenyon Road, Urbana, Illinois 61801

Book Design: Tom Kovacs for TGK Design

NCTE Stock Number 31476

Library of Congress Cataloging in Publication Data

Bartel, Roland.
   Metaphors and symbols.

   Includes bibliographical references.
   1. Metaphor. I. Title
PN228.M4B37   1983   809   83–10623
ISBN 0–8141–3147–6

Contents

Preface

I am convinced that the study of metaphor should not be limited to the metaphors of poetry. When we expand that study to include the full range of metaphors, we introduce students to the most dynamic aspects of language and help them to see the metaphors of poetry in new perspective. To achieve this result we must go far beyond the material on metaphor found in most textbooks and try to understand the significance of metaphors wherever we find them.

I have relied upon a large number of examples from a variety of sources because I find examples indispensable in teaching metaphor and symbol. Although most of these examples can be incorporated into class discussions and used in developing assignments, I have also included specific exercises and practical teaching suggestions in several sections of the book.

In the final chapter I discuss the humanistic aspects of metaphor and symbol and try to explain why it is worthwhile and necessary to present these aspects as completely as possible. Although this material is more theoretical than what precedes it, I consider it to be the foundation for everything else. I believe that our ability to make and use metaphor has profound implications for our teaching; as William Carlos Williams puts it in "A Sort of Song," we should be able "through metaphor to reconcile the people and the stones."

I am happy to acknowledge that a grant from the Oregon Committee for the Humanities was very helpful in preparing this manuscript.

Metaphors and Symbols

1 Popular Metaphor

A comprehensive approach to metaphor might well begin with a review of popular metaphor. Such an approach demonstrates the pervasiveness and importance of metaphors and provides students with a useful background for studying the metaphors of poetry.

To get to the many interesting aspects of metaphor as quickly as possible, we might begin with the briefest possible working definition of metaphor—any comparison that cannot be taken literally—and postpone the consideration of simile and other related topics. This simple definition is all we need to acquaint students with the human trait that generates most of our metaphors, namely, our fascination with unusual comparisons. As we survey the vast field of popular metaphor, we will discover how universal is our delight in unexpected comparisons, especially when these comparisons transcend the limitations of literal language. As Ralph Waldo Emerson wrote in "Poetry and Imagination," "When some familiar truth or fact appears in a new dress, mounted as on a fine horse, equipped with a grand pair of ballooning wings, we cannot enough testify our surprise and pleasure. It is like the new virtue in some unprized old property, as when a boy finds that his pocketknife will attract steel filings and take up a needle." It is worth noting that Emerson used six comparisons to describe the thrill produced by comparisons. Let us examine how comparisons affect our language and our lives today to see whether Emerson's rhapsodies remain valid.

In Riddles

That metaphorical comparisons have provided amusement for people in all parts of the world for centuries is demonstrated by the intriguing riddles preserved in the traditional literature of many countries. Of special value in this connection are the riddles found in Maria Leach's *Riddle Me, Riddle Me, Ree* (Viking, 1970), Loretta Burke Hubp's *Qué Será: What Can It Be? Traditional Spanish Riddles* (John Day, 1970), and Archer Taylor's *English Riddles from Oral Tradition* (University of California Press, 1951; Octagon Books, 1977). Although these riddles have interesting cultural and psychological implications, their greatest significance for the teaching of metaphor lies in the simple beauty of their imaginative comparisons.

In Spanish traditional riddles the moon has been called a little white mare that leaps over hills and ravines with no harm coming to it, a rib that becomes a tortilla, a piece of bread tossed on a vast pampa, and a beautiful woman in a dress of gold who turns her face now to this side, now to the other. In English traditional riddles the moon is a pumpkin in a meadow, a deer that walks alone, a pancake that travels, sour milk in a cup, a bucket, a cup, and a white yam. In other riddles the moon is a white mare in a lake (Ireland), a bald man looking under a gate (Russia), one big fish in a great big pond (Africa), and a long thin boat that becomes a plate (Burma). The crescent moon has been called a crust of bread hanging over an old woman's hut, out of the reach of barking dogs (Russia).

The sun has been called a great mirror that lights the world (Cape Verde Islands) and a silver dish floating in the middle of the sea (Siberia). The rising sun is a red cock crowing on a roof (Norway), and the sun and the moon are two white cows lying in a farmyard—one during the day and the other at night (Ireland). The night sky is a great field full of geese and one gander (Wales); a basket that is empty in the morning and full of flowers at night (Ceylon); a thousand lights in a dish (India); and a field that cannot be measured, filled with sheep that cannot be counted, herded by a shepherd with two horns (Russia). Night and day are a black and a white horse chasing each other forever in vain (Iran), a black cow that knocks down all the people and a white cow that makes them get up (Russia), and a black bull that pulls out the little white bull that has fallen into the sea (Spain.)

Snow is a white glove on the window sill (England), a snowdrift is a white scarf across the gate (Russia), and a snowflake is a featherless bird from Paradise dying in one's hand (Shetland Islands). Rain is likened to the arrows of God that cannot be counted (Philippine Islands), and a cloud is someone who grows fat without eating (Babylon). In Spanish traditional riddles a clouded sky is a patched quilt that doesn't have a single stitch, lightning is a brilliant bird that flashes over the sea, and fog is strands of white hair floating between two ravines.

In English traditional riddles bows and arrows are humpbacked mothers with straight children, and a frying pan is a little sister who cries louder the more she is fed. A fire in the kitchen with smoke outside is a mule in a stable with its tail outside, but a sunbeam is a white mare's tail that has been forced through the window.

The makers of these riddles deserve to be called folk poets for a number of reasons. They like to play with images, they delight in seeing one thing in terms of another, they have an intuitive sense of the interrelationship of things, they are willing to attempt daring comparisons, and they challenge us to see the familiar in a new light. For the most part, the metaphors in riddles do little more than produce enjoyable images, which is also a primary function of the metaphors in poetry, but occasionally the metaphors in riddles combine new images with significant implications and in that way take on features of more complex metaphors, as when writing is compared to scattering black seeds on white land (England), the tongue and teeth are compared to a snake guarded by soldiers (England), a man's head is compared to a clod of earth with seven holes (India), the human heart trying to recall the past is likened to someone digging about a deserted village (Africa), and ashes are described as the dead burying the living (England).

In Folk Expressions and Proverbs

Our fascination with the comparisons that make up our simplest metaphors is also reflected in the vast number of popular expressions that have become a permanent part of our language. Though not as engaging as the metaphors of riddles, folk expressions are important for the study of metaphor because of their sheer pervasiveness. The fact that some of these folk expressions are hundreds of years old is a tribute to the power of comparisons—they are not destroyed by cultural changes. "Bring home the bacon," for example, goes back to the twelfth century when the bacon was literally a prize given to a couple who hadn't quarreled in a year. A survey of these expressions reveals that they have their origin in every period of history, from biblical and classical times to the present. Their ubiquitous nature establishes one important aspect of language, namely, that every generation seems to delight in making new comparisons to express old ideas.

Very helpful in this connection are three books that trace popular folk sayings back to their origins: Charles Earle Funk's *A Hog on Ice and Other Curious Expressions* (Harper and Row, 1948), his *Heavens to Betsy and Other Curious Sayings* (Harper and Row, 1955), and Alfred H. Holt's *Phrase Origins* (Crowell, 1936). These books record interesting stories about some of our stalest expressions. What these stories reveal is that folk expressions have migrated through three stages: they began as literal terms, they were converted into metaphors to express an old idea in a novel way, and they again became literal when the metaphors were destroyed through overuse. The final literal meaning, however, differs from the first one because it is derived from the intervening metaphorical stage. Although these expressions no longer strike us as metaphors, they began as fresh comparisons, as we can see when we look at their literal origins. Consider, for example, the familiar expression *pin money*. When pins were invented in the fourteenth century, they were so valuable that wives received a special allowance to buy them. The term then became a metaphor for other kinds of extra money, the meaning it retains in its present literal form. A similar cycle can be projected for each of the following expressions.

Cold shoulder. When a host served a cold shoulder of mutton to a guest, it was clear that the host had made no advance preparation. The guest obviously wasn't appreciated enough to be served a warm meal.

Potluck. Going home with someone and partaking in whatever by luck was in the pot.

Going to pot. In a foundry, refuse metal and other scraps were thrown into a stewing pot. Variant origins are death by cannibals who put their victims into a pot or putting the ashes of the dead into urns.

Seamy side. The wrong side, the underside with the seams that we try to hide from view.

Seedy. Weak or worn out, like a plant gone to seed.

Pull strings. From the manipulation of marionettes or jointed puppets.

Become unhinged. From doors taken off their hinges.

Eavesdropper. One who hangs from the eaves of a roof near an open window to find out what is happening in a house; one who stands near a window under the drip from the eaves.

Dead as a doornail. Refers to the knob on which a door knocker strikes. It is thought to be dead because of the number of blows it has received.

Skinflint. Stingy, miserly—one who would skin flint if that were possible.

Brush up. Comes from reviving a fire by stirring out the ashes, brushing up the hearth.

Kick the bucket. From Elizabethan days, one hanged oneself by kicking out the bucket on which one stood.

Bury the hatchet. From the American Indian custom of burying hatchets, scalping knives, and war clubs when a war ended so that the war could be forgotten.

Let the cat out of the bag. People who bought suckling pigs in sacks were often cheated by being given a cat instead. If they opened the sack before paying, they would let the cat out of the bag and avoid being cheated. If they did not open the sack, they bought a pig in a poke (an archaic term for sack).

Clincher. From the practice of clinching nails so they cannot be easily pulled out.

Raking someone over the coals. Refers to the old practice of extorting money from Jews by hauling them over the coals of a fire until they agreed to pay.

Sold down the river. Selling slaves via auctions from worn-out tobacco farms and sending them down the river to more prosperous tobacco farms.

Coach. At first a tutor, someone who helped a student move ahead (like the vehicle); now a term more commonly used in athletics.

Copper. A policeman because he "cops" or catches people. From the Latin *capere* (to take, seize), the *a* having been corrupted to an *o*.

Crocodile tears. From the belief that crocodiles shed tears while they ate their victims.

Cut and dried. From curing hay or timber.

Have one's work cut out. Tailors used to cut out garments and give them to others in the shop to make into clothes.

Earmarked. From the practice of marking the ears of sheep and cattle for identification.

Making both ends meet. A rope must be long enough to go around whatever is being tied up; the ends of the rope must meet.

Laugh up one's sleeve. Goes back to the time when people wore sleeves that were so large that they could hide their faces in their sleeves while they were laughing.

To a T. Refers to the accuracy of the T square used by carpenters. Variantly, short for "to a tittle," the small sign used as a diacritical marking in printing.

Touch and go. In a near collision, cars or ships may barely touch and keep on going.

Lick something into shape. Based on an old belief that bear cubs were born shapeless and had to be licked into shape by mamma bear.

Not dry behind the ears. When a colt or calf is born, the last spot to dry is the area behind the ears, hence, someone newly born— naive and credulous.

In the bag. The merchandise is in the bag, ready for delivery. Before the advent of bags, the expression was "all wrapped up."

Come to the end of one's rope. Animals staked for grazing are limited by the length of the rope. Alternately, a reference to the hangman's rope and the end of one's life.

Get the brush-off. To be treated like lint that has to be brushed off. The expression may also refer to the actions of a porter who, suspecting a small tip, gives a person just a few flicks of the brush.

Be on the beam. Refers to radio beams directing airplane travel.

Sucker. A dupe or simpleton as naive as a young animal that still sucks.

Fly off the handle. Losing one's temper as suddenly as an axe head flies off the handle.

To this list might be added those clichés with literal-metaphorical origins that are self-explanatory: putting the cart before the horse, keeping the pot boiling, being in hot water, hitting the nail on the head, striking while the iron is hot, turning a new leaf, swallowing something hook, line and sinker. We should also note that Aesop's fables have provided us with such popular metaphors as dog in the manger, sour grapes, wolf in sheep's clothing, crying wolf, blowing hot and cold, the lion's share, the hare and the tortoise, and the goose that laid the golden egg.

The literal-metaphorical-literal cycle is especially transparent in folk expressions that have become proverbs: chickens will come home to roost, a new broom sweeps clean, look before you leap, a stitch in time saves nine, make hay while the sun shines, when the cat's away the mice will play, don't put all your eggs in one basket, and many others. We should note in passing that not all proverbs are eroded metaphors. Those in which abstract concepts were not translated into concrete terms have always been literal: honesty is the best policy, haste makes waste, practice what you preach, every little bit helps, a soft answer turneth away wrath ("turneth" is no longer metaphorical), nothing ventured nothing gained.

In Clichés

Ironically, one of the best sources for teaching the vitality of metaphors may be dead metaphors—the thousands of clichés that once began as comparisons. Whereas folk expressions often survive as compressed anecdotes, clichés are the less picturesque words and phrases based on short, transparent comparisons that are quickly eroded by repetition. Though clichés have a short metaphorical life, they seldom forget their metaphorical origins. Because of their tenacity, their number keeps growing, and they may well constitute the largest reservoir of implied metaphors in the language. We might alert students to the universality of clichés by giving one or two examples in various categories and encouraging them to extend the list. We should remind them that to qualify as metaphor/cliché an expression must show evidence that it is used outside its original category, for example, "flight plan" used in a context other than aviation or "spinning my wheels" used outside the field of transportation.

Consider, for example, how readily we have used the language of sports metaphorically outside the field of sports: jump the gun, touch all bases, caught off base, throw in the towel, carry the ball, clear the hurdle, out in left field, on the last lap, throw a curve, behind the eight ball, fish in troubled waters, swim against the current, have a game plan. Conversely, consider how sports writers import metaphors from other fields: beanball, horsehide, shutout, whitewash, hot box, windup, choke in the clutch, cauliflower ear.

Consider also how the parts of our body have provided metaphors in a variety of fields: foot of a mountain, brow of a hill, eye of a needle, tongue of a wagon, tongue in cheek, cold feet, rule of thumb, tooth and nail, shoulder of the road, hands of a clock, mouth of a river, well-heeled, down at the heels, down at the mouth, keeping one's feet on the ground, having one's nose out of joint, save face, lose face, foot in the mouth, teeth on edge, stiff upper lip, skin of one's teeth, thumbs down, thumb a ride, burning one's fingers, keeping people on their toes, stepping on their toes.

Or consider how the names of animals provide us with metaphors that serve as various parts of speech. People wolf their food, outfox their enemies, horse around, and cow their inferiors; they doggedly pursue their studies; the stock market is bearish or bullish and people tell fishy stories, shed crocodile tears, and become henpecked. A person may be a hawk, a dove, a lamb, a chicken, or a goose; a person may be a lame duck, a dead duck, or an ugly duckling; not to mention a mouse, a rat, a snake in the grass, a mule, a goat, or a vulture.

In Literal Words

When we consider that many folk expressions and clichés have found their way into standard dictionaries, we cannot avoid an obvious question: Are there other words in dictionaries that began as metaphors? To answer this question we must make a distinction between literal and metaphorical expressions.

Literal language refers to the definitions found in dictionaries. Since dictionaries are made for the general public, they contain only those definitions that have received significant public approval. The definitions are literal because of this general agreement about their meaning. We can use them and expect to be understood because their meanings have become standardized through repetition and consensus. Literal definitions, then, are dictionary definitions.

Metaphors, on the other hand, are not found in dictionaries because they are expressions designed to communicate new insights. Newness is the essence of metaphor; we invent them when we find literal language too dull or too restrictive for what we have to say. We invent a metaphor when we give a word a meaning not found in a dictionary. Every time we do this we make a comparison; we say in effect that the literal meaning of a word can be transferred to a new category with which it shares certain traits. Thus we have taken the literal meaning of the word *door*—an entrance into a building or room—and transferred it to new categories in which the comparison is obvious: doors (access) to opportunity, to education, to careers. The metaphorical uses of *door* have become so prevalent that one dictionary considers them literal and includes among its definitions "a means of access" and gives as an example "door to success." Keeping in mind this distinction between literal and metaphorical language, we can return to our question about the role of metaphor in the formation of literal vocabulary.

If we examine just about any page of a dictionary, we discover that nearly every word has several meanings. How did this happen? If we look closely at the multiple meanings of just about any word, we find at least a partial answer. Most of the definitions contain traces of worn-out comparisons and are, like the definition of *door* above, eroded metaphors. This basic fact about language can be illustrated with thousands of examples, but I will limit myself to only a few.

According to the *Oxford English Dictionary*, the word *groom* first meant a boy, then a man of inferior position, and then a servant who attends horses. When *groom* became a verb to describe the way a horse is curried and trained for a race, the word acquired picturesque qualities that were badly needed to describe preparations in other fields. With no trouble at all, *groom* was transferred from its literal category of caring for horses to such metaphorical categories as preparing students for careers, athletes for contests, and politicians for campaigns. As the new uses of the word were repeated, they became generally accepted and were added to the original, literal meanings of the word.

The word *groom* has become especially popular in politics, probably because we have converted so many other terms from horse racing into political metaphors: a political contest is frequently called a horse race; a close contest may be neck and neck, go down to the wire, be won by a nose, or end in a photo finish by the candidate having the inside track. A weak candidate is a long shot and may soon be out of the running and become an also-ran. A candidate who differs substantially from other candidates or from the first impression he or she created is a horse of a different color. The strongest candidate becomes the front runner and will probably be a shoo-in, provided he or she curries favor with the voters and enough people put their money on that candidate. The candidate with hidden potential is a dark horse, and the one who bolts the party is like the horse that bolts or breaks away from a rider's control.

Not all metaphorical uses of *bolt* derive from horse racing, however. An arrow and a streak of lightning are also called bolts, and the suddenness and the speed of their motion makes *bolt* an appropriate metaphor to describe an unexpected happening (a bolt out of the blue), unseemly haste (bolting one's food), or a sudden or premature start (vegetables bolting to seed, horses and candidates bolting into a race). When Australians call a fugitive from justice a bolter, the meaning is clear even though we cannot be sure whether the metaphor came from horse racing, from lightning, from arrows, or from all three. Whatever the explanation, it is clear that we have no difficulty in transferring from one category to another those words that we find most appealing and then allowing the new metaphorical meanings to become literal through repetition.

Other examples tell a similar story. *Backbone* originally meant the vertebral column of the human body, and then it was transferred to other areas to suggest such qualities as stability and strength and support. A metal frame becomes the backbone of a bicycle, a mountain range the backbone of a country, star players the backbone of the team, civic leaders the backbone of the community, and someone with a strong character a person with moral backbone. When the term was overused to describe admirable people, it was replaced with fresher metaphors, many of them also transferred from parts of the body. A courageous person has nerve, guts, a stout heart, a strong stomach; conversely, a coward is spineless, gutless, or unnerved and has cold feet, a soft head, a faint heart, a chicken heart, a chicken liver, or a white liver.

Other compounds built from *back* have lent themselves to metaphorical transfers almost as readily as *backbone*. *Backlog* began literally as the large log in the back of a fireplace, where it burned slowly and provided a reserve of heat for a long period of time, sometimes through the entire night. Soon other reserves became known as backlogs: business orders, extra provisions of all kinds, and accumulations of various emotions, such as a backlog of good will or hatred. *Backdoor* is defined literally in *OED* as a door in the back of a building, a secondary or private entrance; figuratively it is defined as unworthily secret or clandestine. The latter definition adds color to one of the better sports metaphors of recent years, the backdoor pass in basketball which results in an easy score. When a backdoor pass succeeds, the opposition has every reason to regard it as being as secret and clandestine as backdoor diplomacy or as stealthy as entrance through private backdoors.

In Slang

The popular metaphors we have already examined—those in riddles, in folk expressions, in clichés, and in the literal definitions in our dictionaries—would seem to justify the effusions of Emerson concerning comparisons. Our survey of our obsession with comparison would not, however, be complete without considering the extraordinary methods implicit in slang. Walt Whitman called slang "an attempt to escape bald literalism and express itself illimitably, which in highest walks produces poets and poems" (*North American Review*, 1885), and G. K. Chesterton, finding the language of the lower classes to be more original and poetic than the language of the aristocracy, concluded that "all slang is metaphor, and all metaphor is poetry" (*A Defense of Nonsense* (Dodd, Mead, 1911).

Various motives have been ascribed to the makers and users of slang—defiance, secrecy, peer loyalty, economy, self-assertion, creativity—but the most prominent motive is the one most closely related to the motive that inspires riddles, folk expressions, and clichés: the desire for pleasure and variety in language, usually by means of novel comparisons. In riddles the comparisons are ends in themselves, providing entertainment through tests of ingenuity. In folk expressions and clichés the comparisons originally gave new life to old ideas, all within the bounds of standard English. In slang the comparisons are often so strained or so remote that they are hardly noticeable as comparisons, a fact that gives slang its most distinctive qualities. Although the comparisons may be obscure, their vitality is conspicuous.

The makers of slang are free to use words in any way they choose. Since they can ignore the dictionary meaning of words, the rules of grammar, ordinary logic, and common sense, they are able to produce a unique vocabulary that has very little connection with standard English. Depending on their motives and their resourcefulness, they can come up with words that are mysterious or self-explanatory, colorful or drab, shocking or soothing, humorous or dull. But it is the quality and audacity of their coinages that convince us that their primary motive is to counteract monotony and boredom. As Stuart B. Flexner observes in his preface to the second edition of *Dictionary of American Slang* (Crowell, 1975), "Sometimes slang is used to escape the dull familiarity of standard words, to suggest an escape from the established routine of everyday life. When slang is used, our life seems a little fresher and a little more personal. Also, at all levels of speech, slang is sometimes used for the pure joy of making sounds, or even for a need to attract attention by making noise. The sheer newness and informality of certain slang words produces pleasure" (p. xi). In *The American Language, Supplement II* (Knopf, 1948), H. L. Mencken called slang "a delirious delight in language-making" whose "chief aim seems to be to say something new, not necessarily something good" (pp. 644-45).

This desire to find new ways of saying the same thing has produced a slang vocabulary that is truly astounding. To get the full impact of this phenomenon, we need to consult a thesaurus of slang rather than a dictionary of slang, for a thesaurus brings together slang synonyms for a single concept. Although we have many dictionaries of slang, we have at this time only one thesaurus, *The American Thesaurus of Slang* (Crowell, 1953), edited by Lester V. Berrey and Melvin Van den Bark. In spite of its publication date, this book remains valuable for demonstrating the profuseness and diversity of slang. It lists one hundred fifty terms for nonsense (from applesauce to baloney and banana oil, from bunk to crud to horsefeathers, from poppycock to rubbish and stewed rhubarb, tommyrot and whoopla); fifty terms for an old car (ash can, bone crusher, kidney buster, and jalopy, to mention only four); four hundred terms for hot rod and its variants; one hundred eighty terms for having no money (broke and busted, cleaned and clipped, flat as a pancake); four hundred terms for failing (from bit the dust to fall flat, flop, flunk, fold, and foozle to lay an egg or strike out or hit the skids or miss the boat); forty terms to describe decisive defeat (from bury to crush to massacre, from maul to plaster, pulverize, shellac, slaughter, and wipe out); fifty terms for losing one's job (to be axed, booted, bounced, canned, chucked, sacked; to get the gate, a pink slip, or walking papers); two hundred terms for getting angry (from blowing a fuse or a gasket or one's cork or stopper or lid to flying off the handle, having a hemorrhage or kittens or puppies, hitting the ceiling, simmering, sizzling, smoking, smoldering, and stewing).

What is especially significant about these long lists of slang synonyms is that they are not needed for clear, effective communication. Standard English usually provides all the words we need to express ourselves accurately. If we want to say that something is excellent, depending on context and connotation, we can use superior, exceptional, remarkable, great, splendid, unsurpassed, superb, outstanding, magnificent, surpassing, superlative, capital, choice, fine, unexcelled. These are not exact synonyms, and the careful writer or speaker recognizes the subtle differences among them. But precision is of no concern to the makers of slang. They are far more interested in the tinge of humor and the momentary thrill that comes from contriving new ways of saying old things, and so, according to *The American Thesaurus of Slang,* they have coined no fewer than five hundred slang terms to express the notion of excellence: bully, cheesey, corking, creamy, whammy, whopping, to list only a half dozen. And they have extended the list with such feline terms as cat's meow, cat's eyebrows, cat's ankles, cat's tonsils, cat's adnoids, cat's galoshes, cat's pajamas, cat's cuff links, cat's roller skates, and cat's whiskers.

Do we really need five hundred ways of saying cat's whiskers? Yes we do, because the long list reflects a joyous and creative use of language with which we dare not interfere. The list also reflects the transitoriness of slang, another of its virtues, for rapid obsolescence and renewal are the essence of the most exciting aspects of slang. Some slang expressions, however, do survive—some as more or less permanent slang terms, others as acceptable additions to the lexicons of standard English.

Dangerous Metaphors

For years America prided itself as the melting pot of the word. Orators boasted that immigrants from any country whatsoever could be shaped into the American mold. For decades the melting pot metaphor represented the American dream, but when various minorities began to assert their identities, the metaphor became an obstacle to social progress. As minorities insisted that they could be patriotic without giving up their identities, the melting pot metaphor was replaced by such sociological terms as "cultural pluralism." Perhaps the best description of the new attitude toward minorities is contained in the metaphor "cultural mosaic," an inspired term suggesting that a country can be enriched and its unity strengthened by preserving the identity of its diverse ethnic groups.

The power of metaphor is at the heart of a most unusual argument in international affairs, namely, the contention that Winston Churchill is responsible for the Berlin Wall. Those who support that argument believe that when Churchill used the iron curtain metaphor in his speech in Fulton, Missouri, on March 5, 1946, he set in motion such strong feelings about the cold war with Russia that the erection of the wall became inevitable. Even though Churchill was not the first to use the metaphor, he certainly popularized it and gave it power. How much responsibility he has for the Berlin Wall remains an open question, but there can be no question about the ability of a strong metaphor to beguile us and obstruct our thinking, as a few more examples will show.

In the early stages of the Vietnam War, someone justified American intervention in terms of the domino theory, a vivid metaphor describing the danger of letting one country after another fall to the Communists. As time passed, the metaphor became an attractive substitute for thought and kept us from reexamining the basic issues of the war. It was simply too convenient to answer difficult questions with that metaphor. A similar thing happened with the words *hawk* and *dove*. At first they were convenient metaphors for describing two extreme attitudes toward the war, but then they began to polarize discussions of the war, making it difficult to defend any position between the extremes.

One of the most unfortunate recent metaphors is popular with many undergraduates, the student-as-consumer metaphor. The rights of consumers have received so much publicity and support in recent years that students could not resist equating their demands with those of consumers. Those who use this metaphor endanger a basic premise of education. Through it they imply that education is a supermarket where students shop for bargains; gone is the basic concept of education as a cooperative exploration of controversial issues, with findings reported in tentative and qualified terms.

Similar examples of dangerous metaphors based on confused thinking are found in the moral realm, mainly because of the popularity of certain metaphorical proverbs. That you have to fight fire with fire is seldom true on the literal level. Only on rare occasions do forest or prairie fires have to be fought with backfires, but the proverb is so vivid that it is easily remembered and repeated. It has, in fact, become a vicious metaphor used to justify revenge in human relations at all levels—personal, national, and international. Small wonder that Wendell Willkie, candidate for the United States presidency in 1940, observed that a good catchword (in most cases a metaphor) can obscure analytical thinking for fifty years. Fortunately, this kind of destructive power is not typical of most popular metaphors.

Six Conclusions about Popular Metaphors

1. Metaphors that have become clichés are victims of their own popularity. We can assume that they were worn down by repetition because their appeal was so great; their appeal was so great because they provided pleasures and satisfactions not found in literal language. Even those that are considered anathema in written discourse can, if used judiciously, add color and realism to oral discourse. "Having too many irons in the fire" seems almost indispensable for describing people who are a bit disorganized and trying to do too many things at the same time.

2. Triteness is clearly a matter of degree. In its cycle from birth to death, from literal to metaphorical and back to literal, a metaphor passes through several irregular stages. The same metaphor may be stale to one person and fresh to another. Neither is the rate of decline uniform. Most slang metaphors live for only a short time, but some have wide appeal and live for centuries. The metaphor "Does it send you?" inspired by Elvis Presley had a short life, but the comparable metaphor "Does it turn you on?" inspired by the Beatles and the counterculture shows signs of lasting much longer. Some metaphors disappear but others are reborn. "Out of sight" was used in 1895 by Stephen Crane in *Maggie: A Girl of the Streets*. The term disappeared for decades but was recently revived to describe something very good or very bad. It may be related to the jazz metaphor "out of this world."

3. Popular metaphors illustrate the flexibility and growth of language. As metaphors are eroded by their own popularity, they are added to our stock of literal words and are then replaced by new metaphors. When we describe ourselves as being upset about something, we are using a term that has migrated most of the way from the metaphorical to the literal. But when we say we are going to pieces, coming apart at the seams, unhinged or unglued, we are using expressions that are somewhere between the metaphorical and the literal, worn but not yet threadbare. Some metaphors even reverse their meanings. *Square* once had positive connotations, probably because we admire the neatness and precision of a square: square meal, square deal, square shooting, four-square gospel church. Recently the term has become a derogatory epithet applied to old fogies. Long-haired music once referred to classical music only, but the term is now more appropriately applied to rock music. To some students bombing an examination means to fail it, to others it means to pass it.

4. It is obviously easier and more enjoyable to add new meanings to old words than to invent new words. About half of the 100,000 new words and definitions added to our language between the publication of the second (1934) and third (1961) editions of Webster's unabridged dictionary began as metaphors; the other half were made by compounding, a process also based on comparison, albeit comparisons that are much more obvious than those in metaphors (snowmobile, moonwalk, earthrise, doubleknit, hard hat, spin-off).

5. Although popular metaphors are an almost inexhaustible source of pleasure, some have the power to obscure analytical thinking and to deter thoughtful discussion.

6. When we consider how many of the words in a dictionary contain at least one definition that is an eroded comparison, we have reason to suspect that metaphors may be the most important ingredient in the growth of language. It should not shock us that some scholars are now saying that all words began as metaphors, that our language is a necropolis of dead metaphors.

Teaching Suggestions

For Riddles

The purpose of these exercises and of the earlier discussion of riddles is to develop sensitivity to comparisons—their pleasure and their significance—a first step in learning to enjoy and understand metaphor.

1. Ask students to skim books of riddles and bring to class those riddles they find most interesting. They can also ask adults for favorite riddles. Students then sort this collection of riddles: those that contain comparisons and those that don't. Remind them that all personifications contain comparisons. What subcategories for those containing comparisons can be devised?

2. Use the riddles given on pages 3-5 in guessing games. Encourage students to contribute riddle-comparisons of their own creation for sun, moon, snow, night, and day.

3. Ask students to devise riddles based on unusual comparisons. This activity can lead directly to metaphors in poetry, as do similar exercises in Kenneth Koch's two useful books: *Wishes, Lies, and Dreams: Teaching Children to Write Poetry* (Harper and Row, 1980) and *Rose, Where Did You Get That Red? Teaching Great Poetry to Children* (Random House, 1973).

4. Invite students to share their reactions to riddles on page 5 that seem to go beyond mere description. What, for example, is implied in the riddle that compares the tongue and the teeth to a snake guarded by soldiers? In the riddle that compares writing to scattering black seed on white land? In the riddle that describes ashes as the dead burying the living? Advanced students might discuss this last comparison in terms of Shakespeare's sonnet 73, where the way life is destroyed by the aging human body is compared to the way fire is smothered by the ashes of the wood that used to feed it.

5. For good measure, here are more riddles with "poetic" comparisons, including their answers.

> What has been likened to a legless man without a staff who fears ducks and hens but not dogs? (a worm)
>
> What is like ten boys with hats on the back of their heads? (the fingers)
>
> What is like snow that falls on a tree stump but does not melt? (gray hair)
>
> What is like little doors that open and shut without a sound? (eyelids)
>
> What is like a black string in one's path? (a procession of ants)
>
> What is like a man with his trousers rolled to his knees, carrying a saw over his head? (a rooster)

What is like a bird that walks on its beak? (a top)

What travels about a valley, patting its hands like a woman making tortillas? (a butterfly)

What is like a tunnel in a hill which a mule enters with cargo and returns without cargo? (the mouth and a spoon)

6. Finally, we should not overlook the riddle of the Sphinx in Greek mythology: What walks on four legs in the morning, two legs at noon, and three legs at night? Those who did not recognize the comparisons (morning as childhood, noon as middle age, night as old age) could not answer the riddle and were devoured by the Sphinx. Oedipus saved the city of Thebes and caused the Sphinx to destroy herself when he answered correctly that the riddle referred to a person—a baby on all fours, an adult walking erect, and an old person with a cane.

For Folk Expressions

Folk sayings can be used in several ways to demonstrate the metaphorical nature of language.

1. The fact that students find some folk expressions obsolete shows that comparisons come and go from generation to generation. Ask students to collect popular as well as obscure folk expressions from family members and to add their own favorites. Use these in class discussions. Students may discover that expressions common to one family are unheard of in another. Students might also try their hands at providing modern equivalents for expressions no longer used by the younger generation.

2. Scholars do not always agree on the origin or meaning of folk expressions, and these differences of opinion suggest that some comparisons are so vivid that they inspire diverse explanations, not just by scholars but by those who enjoy repeating the expressions. "Driven from pillar to post" has spawned at least five explanations, and "flash in the pan" and "dead as a doornail" have also been explained in several ways. Why not ask students to invent explanations of their own for folk expressions, encouraging them to approach these comparisons from both a logical and a fanciful point of view.

3. Ask students to write a paragraph or a paper on characteristics of interesting folk expressions—concreteness, areas of human activity from which the comparisons are drawn, and the like.

4. And here are additional folk expressions with metaphorical comparisons that can be used in writing assignments and class discussions.

Wild goose chase. Wild geese were hard to catch and almost worthless when they were caught.

Fleece a person. Defraud, as when sheep lose their fleece to shearers.

His name is mud. Dr. Samuel Mudd received a life sentence for setting the broken leg of John Wilkes Booth, Lincoln's assassin. Although Dr. Mudd was pardoned after four years by President Andrew Johnson, his action inspired the derogatory saying. In July, 1979, Mudd's descendants obtained a letter from President Carter clearing Dr. Mudd of guilt, but will the letter kill the popular saying?

Read between the lines. Secret messages were sometimes sent in invisible ink between the visible lines of an innocent letter.

Bang-up job. As successful as a display of banging fireworks.

Woolgathering. Doing nothing especially worthwhile, as children sent to gather wool from hedges where sheep had passed.

Scot-free. Tax-free, *scot* originally meaning tax.

Posthaste. To travel rapidly, as did the relays of post horses.

Harping on something. Like a harpist who plays the same string over and over again.

Where do you hang out? Businesses and residences used to hang out identifying signs, now humorously referred to as shingles (cf. *pad*).

Armed to the teeth. Armed so heavily that an additional weapon, like a knife, had to be carried between the teeth.

Beat the band. Make enough noise to drown out the band.

Land-office business. Real estate offices were extremely busy when new territories were opened in the West.

Steal one's thunder. Playwrights accused their rivals of stealing or imitating the devices for producing thunder offstage.

Weasel words. Weasels can suck eggs without breaking them, hence, empty words.

Led by the nose. Animals are easily controlled if led by the nose.

Called on the carpet. When servants were to be reprimanded, they had to stand on a carpet placed before their master or mistress.

Bite the dust. A slain person bites the dust when he hits the ground.

Beside the mark. Bowmen who can't hit the target in archery.

Handwriting on the wall. Warnings and omens, as in the book of Daniel.

Pull up stakes. Refers to boundary stakes.

Old stamping ground. Places where animals and later people gathered.

Put one's shoulder to the wheel. Help a horse pull a cart out of the mud or up a hill.

Over the barrel. Nearly drowned persons used to be laid over a barrel for resuscitation.

Get it in the neck. Refers to the way chickens are killed for eating.

Throw the book at someone. The maximum punishment, all the rules in the book.

Keep your shirt on. Fighters used to remove their shirts before fighting.

Sailing under false colors. Pirates changed flags to avoid attack.

Left high and dry. Like a ship stranded on a sandbar.

Low man on the totem pole. The figure carved at the bottom of the pole seems to bear the weight of all those carved above.

Feel one's oats. A horse full of oats often displays its energy.

For Clichés

Clichés may be the most neglected resource for teaching metaphor. Since they are so numerous and so accessible, we can use them to illustrate many aspects of metaphor.

1. Ask students to collect comparisons from sports pages. Ask them to consider why sports writers use so many clichés. One writer told me that clichés are more interesting than words that are completely literal. Is that always true?

A recent sports page contained these cliché substitutes for a batter getting a hit: poked a double, smacked a single, cracked a single, lashed a double, powered a home run, ripped two home runs, launched two home runs. On the same page one team ended a drought, another snapped a losing streak, a third broke a winning streak, another completed a four-game sweep, and a fifth hung on to win. A broadcast of a single football game contained these cliché metaphors that students might be asked to analyze: blitz the quarterback, sack the quarterback, push the quarterback out of the pocket, shotgun formation, players who are really pumped up, a quarterback who had to eat the ball or cough it up or dump it off, a quarterback's pass that was on the money, a game that was a barnburner with lots of fireworks in the second half, a halfback who whistled through a seam in the line, a bread-and-butter play, a flea-flicker play, a team stoked up and ripping off big yards (big chunks) and grinding out the yards.

2. Headlines also can be gleaned for clichés to analyze: President Clears Path for Grain Sales to Russia, Controls Draw Fire, Sugar Quotas Hit, Decaying Buildings Need Dentistry. Headline writers, like sports reporters, apparently consider clichés more appealing than literal language.

3. Popular similes quickly become clichés, as any collection of similes readily demonstrates to students. See, for example, Grenville Kleiser, *Similes and Their Use* (Dunlap, 1925; Richard West, 1973) and Frank L. Wilstach, *A Dictionary of Similes* (Little, Brown, 1916; Adler, 1969). Students will be surprised to discover how easy it is to make new similes if they are innovative in completing just about any comparison: happy as, cold as, smooth as, hungry as. The spring, 1979, issue of *Foxfire* lists many worn similes still popular in rural Georgia.

Similes least likely to degenerate into clichés are those with the most audacious comparisons. T. Hilding Svartengren's *Intensifying Similes In English* (AMS Press, 1918) was first published in Lund, Sweden. The examples in his collection that still seem relatively fresh are those that have not lent themselves to routine repetition: joyful as the back of a gravestone, proud as a dog with side pockets, quiet as a wasp in your nose, handsome as last year's corpse, subtle as a dead pig, dull as a bachelor beaver, chaste as a dog at a bitch-watch, mean as a rooster in a thunder shower.

4. For a humorous treatment of clichés, refer students to Joseph W. Valentine's *Book of Clichés* (Vanguard Press, 1963). There James L. Mackey has provided full-page illustrations for sixty of our stalest clichés. Why not ask students to illustrate clichés or to jumble or reverse them? Clover Adams, the wife of Henry Adams, once observed

about Henry James, "It's not that he 'bites off more than he can chaw' . . ., but he chaws more than he bites off." (Cited on page 272 of Otto Friedrich's *Clover*, Simon and Schuster, 1979.)

Some writers have learned to emphasize a point by taking a cliché literally. When Martin Luther King was told that Negroes should learn to pull themselves up by their bootstraps, he remarked that they could not do that because they had no boots. In one of her columns Abigal Van Buren (Dear Abby) observed that those who fight fire with fire end up with nothing but ashes.

5. Here are additional popular clichés that can be used to remind students of the universality of comparisons and to prepare them for the originality of poetic metaphors. Ask students to identify the hidden comparisons and to discuss their effectiveness.

cut the apron strings	live on a shoe string
wait till the dust settles	the shoe is on the other foot
traffic jam	hold your horses
in the dog house	underdog
get the ax	a leap in the dark
get canned	get a pink slip
get the sack	get walking papers
that's the way the ball bounces	be sent packing
fly the coop	that's the way the cookie crumbles
hit the sack	hit the hay
bent out of shape	sack out
burn one's fingers	nose out of joint
ticket scalpers	make a splash
zero in	an unvarnished lie

6. Finally, remind students that reliance on clichés is a form of mental laziness, a point developed entertainingly by May Swenson in her poem "A Cliché" in *Psyche: The Feminine Poetic Consciousness: An Anthology of Modern American Women Poets*, edited by Barbara Segnitz and Carol Rainey (Dell, 1973). "Is toast," she challenges, "the warmest thing you know?" She urges us to think again: it might even be the "lacy shawl of new-fallen snow."

For Literal Words

The material in this section is crucial for the understanding of metaphor and deserves as much discussion as possible.

1. I recommend at least one assignment asking students to leaf through a dictionary and copy several definitions in which they recognize worn-out comparisons. Every page should provide examples, but if you prefer to assign a few good prospects to each student, here are suggestions.

adrift	cradle	flat	mouth
anchor	dig	fold	nail
apron	digest	ghost	narrow
bend	dim	grasp	neck
brew	dip	ground	needle
browbeat	dirt	hammer	nip
burn	dish	heal	nose
carve	dive	heart	peg
catch	dodge	hitch	pin
chew	door	hollow	pinch
chisel	edge	iron	plunge
choke	elbow	jump	pump
clinch	embrace	kick	raise
cloud	enter	lame	raw
cook	epidemic	lap	ride
cool	explode	leap	road
corner	fire	link	rough
couch	fish	lip	saddle
cough	flame	melt	shadow

2. The editors of the *Oxford English Dictionary* use the labels "figurative" and "transferred" to designate meanings they consider more metaphorical than literal. The fact that most of these definitions appear without these labels in other dictionaries is additional evidence of the movement of words from metaphorical to literal meanings. See, for example, definitions in the *OED* for such words as arid, bait, bald, bitter, blank, boil, cradle, crook, flat, high, low, saddle, shallow, splinter, storm, swallow, varnish, whitewash, wooden, wrestle, and yellow.

3. Students might also examine lists of new words to observe the metaphorical process at work. Good collections of new words are available in the following books:

Annual *Yearbook* supplements to *World Book Encyclopedia,* usually the section preceding the index.

Barnhart Dictionary of New English since 1963, covering the period 1963–73; *Second Barnhart Dictionary of New English,* covering the period 1973–1980. Both books are published by Harper and Row.

6,000 Words: A Supplement to Webster's Third New International Dictionary (Merriam-Webster, 1976) incorporates and expands the eight-page addenda to the 1966 edition of the unabridged dictionary and the sixteen-page addenda of the 1971 edition.

4. Exercises based on the list below will demonstrate to students that many of our most common words have gone through the same literal-metaphorical-literal process that we observed in connection with folk expressions. Students might look these up in dictionaries and other reference books to see whether the literal-metaphorical origin is apparent in the definitions.

Crestfallen. Gamecocks were believed to have erect crests in victory and fallen crests in defeat.

Free lance. In the Middle Ages, some knights were free to hire themselves and their lances to anyone in need of their services.

Blackmail. A tribute exacted by freebooting Scottish chiefs for immunity from pillage, hence extortion (cf. *hush money*).

Bootlegger. During the prohibition era smugglers sometimes hid bottles in their boots.

Chicken feed. Chickens can eat only small objects, hence, small change, paltry sum.

Chip in. From the poker term.

Claptrap. Something added merely to win applause, hence, nonsense.

Diggings or *digs.* Place for mining, then one's home.

Freewheeling. Around 1900 coaster brakes were added to bicycles, permitting wheels to turn without the aid of pedals.

Haywire. A farmer's haywire can become hopelessly entangled.

Salad days. Cool and green and youthful, like fresh salad.

Turncoat. A coat with one color on the inside and another on the outside so it could be turned to match the colors of an approaching enemy.

Ham actors. Inferior actors who had to use ham fat instead of cold cream to remove their makeup.

Well-heeled. Not down at the heels, rich enough to afford new heels.

Seventh heaven. The highest heaven in Islamic religion (cf. *cloud nine*).

Hogwash. The swill fed to swine.

Bigwig. In the eighteenth century, important people wore huge wigs.

Enthrall. Originally it meant enslave, a thrall being a slave.

Big wheel. Probably refers to the big rear wheel that gives a locomotive its power.

Fired up. From keeping a steam engine on a railroad fired up and ready to go.

5. Concordances can also be used to provide a word pool for exercises that teach the difference between literal and metaphorical uses of the same word. The following quotations from the Bible are from the Revised Standard Version except for those marked KJV (King James Version).

The word *kindle* is always literal when used with fire, always metaphorical when used with such abstractions as anger, wrath, and breath.

> You shall kindle no fire . . . on the sabbath day. (Exod. 35:3)
>
> Jacob's anger was kindled against Rachel. (Gen. 30:2)
>
> The anger of the Lord was kindled against Moses. (Exod. 4:14)
>
> He has kindled His wrath against me. (Job 19:11)

The word *pour* is literal when used with water and oil but metaphorical when used with such concepts as indignation, praise, complaint, fame, spirit, wickedness, prayer, grief, lust, contempt, and speech.

> Samuel took a vial of oil, and poured it on his [Saul's] head. (I Sam. 10:1)
>
> Hannah answered . . . I have drunk neither wine nor strong drink, but I have been pouring out my soul before the Lord. (I Sam. 1:15)
>
> I will pour out on the house of David . . . the spirit of compassion. (Zech. 12:10)

I will pour out my thoughts to you. (Prov. 1:23)

Pour out your heart before Him. God is a refuge for us. (Ps. 62:8)

Let the skies pour down righteousness. (Isa. 45:8 KJV)

The word *shepherd* is literal when its use is synonymous with sheepherder; all other uses are metaphorical. *Knit* is always used metaphorically in the Bible. Perhaps its most eloquent use occurs in the description of the closeness of two devoted friends: "The soul of Jonathan was knit to the soul of David, and Jonathan loved him as his own soul" (I Sam. 18:1).

The words *sowing* and *reaping* are literal in the historical and ceremonial books but figurative in the poetic and prophetic books.

As I have seen, those who plow iniquity and sow trouble reap the same. (Job 4:8)

May those who sow in tears reap with shouts of joy. (Ps. 126:5)

For they sow the wind and reap the whirlwind. (Hos. 8:7)

Do not be deceived; God is not mocked, for whatever a man sows, that will he also reap. For he who sows to his own flesh will from the flesh reap corruption; but he who sows to the Spirit will from the Spirit reap eternal life. (Gal. 6:7-8)

The central idea in the above metaphors, that for every effect there is a cause and vice versa, is also expressed in a number of analogies that have metaphorical effects: If A produces B in one realm it will do so with equal certainty in another realm.

Can a man carry fire in his bosom and his clothes not be burned? Or can one walk upon hot coals and his feet not be scorched? So is he who goes in to his neighbor's wife; none who touches her will go unpunished. (Prov. 6:27-29)

The north wind brings rain; and a backbiting tongue, angry looks. (Prov. 25:23)

As charcoal to hot embers and wood to fire so is a quarrelsome man for kindling strife. (Prov. 26:20-21)

Sword is used literally when David abandoned his sword and relied on his slingshot (I Sam. 17:39-51). It is used symbolically in the following passage: "And they shall beat their swords into plowshares, and their spears into pruning hooks; nation shall not lift up sword against nation, neither shall they learn war any more" (Mic. 4:3; Isa. 2:4). It is used as simile and/or metaphor in the following examples because an element of comparison is retained.

His words were softer than oil, yet they were drawn swords. (Ps. 55:20-21)

There are those whose teeth are swords, whose teeth are knives, to devour the poor from off the earth, the needy from among men. (Prov. 30:14)

Boil is used literally when applied to preparing food or heating water, as when Jacob boiled pottage (Gen. 25:29). It is used figuratively only twice:

He makes the deep boil like a pot; he makes the sea like a pot of ointment. (Job 41:31)

My bowels boiled, and rested not: the days of affliction prevented me. (Job 30:27 KJV)

Walk is nearly always metaphorical. Those who live honestly walk in integrity, those who do wrong walk in darkness, those who follow the advice of their teachers are given this promise: "When you walk, your step will not be hampered: and if you run, you will not stumble" (Prov. 4:12).

Concordances to Shakespeare and Emily Dickinson are especially productive for the study of metaphor; however, the most popular metaphors of most authors can be found more quickly in the larger books of quotations. Incidentally, the word *like*, which is omitted in most concordances, is included in Strong's concordance to the Bible, giving us a long list of biblical similes.

For Slang

"Nothing is as old as yesterday's slang" is a popular saying worth remembering. Students should have no trouble providing examples of slang expressions with a very short life. They might be impressed by the fact that articles about the obsolescence of slang inevitably become just as dated as slang itself. On August 17, 1970, *Time* published an article on the changes occurring in slang at that time. The writer noted that *groovy* and *cool* had been resurrected from the 1940s but were again taboo; that *doing your thing, telling it like it is,* and *where it's at* had become "unspeakable for those who would sound current," that any protester shouting "right on" would be considered right off; that *dude* had replaced *cat* and *stud* as a complimentary term for men; that a *freak* was a good person, the opposite of a *square* (p. 32).

H. J. Boyle of the Associated Press observed on June 30, 1952, that "a teenager has to keep up on his slang. At the moment something that used to be known as the cat's whiskers is now called 'sly, really neat, the real George,' or 'deadly boo'" (*Dictionary of American Slang*, second edition, p. 92). This dictionary is a valuable resource for teaching metaphor, but schools with censorship problems may prefer the abridged paperback edition because it omits the most objectionable slang terms, *The Pocket Dictionary of American Slang* (Pocket Books, 1968).

On December 30, 1916, *The New Republic* printed a letter from Mildred Focht, noting that for the "true lover of slang . . . a phrase is taboo after one repetition . . . Once it was my privilege to know a college youth who told me sadly that he could not use slang because it was impossible for him to keep up with the changing styles; so he perforce spoke in correct English." This observation refers, of course, to the most ephemeral kind of slang. There are many degrees of durability among slang terms, or we would not have the tributes to slang cited earlier or such statements as the following from William J. Burke's useful bibliography, *The Literature of Slang* (New York Public Library, 1939; Gale Research, 1965).

> Slang was invented as an antidote to grammar. The rigid formalism of the schools was tempered by the gay and sometimes ribald democracy of street slang, that unconventional and undisciplined language of irreverent youth. Some of these picturesque expressions found their way into the chaste pages of the dictionaries, but not until they had been fumigated. In eugenics it is commonly asserted that the marriage of blue-blooded aristocracy with red-blooded peasant stock keeps a nation sturdy, and in like manner slang brings new blood to a language eternally threatened with over-refinement. Slang keeps the language fresh and flexible . . . slang is fundamentally a state of mind, a manifestation of man's inherent sense of humor and satire, that everpresent corrective for prudery, snobbishness and hypocrisy (p. viii).

Maurice H. Weseen called slang "the probationary period of language" (p. vii in *A Dictionary of American Slang*, Crowell, 1934), and on his title page cited Carl Sandburg's statement that "slang is language that takes off its coat, spits on its hands, and goes to work." Eric Partridge in *Slang Today and Yesterday* (Routledge and Kegan Paul, 1933) listed fifteen reasons why people use slang. His list can be consolidated and summarized as follows: to deflate pomposity, to identify with one's social and occupational groups, to assert one's individuality and ingenuity, to mollify the cruelty of death and other uncertainties of life, to deal concretely with the abstract and the ideal, to find fresh alternatives to clichés and drabness, and to have fun with words (pp. 6–7).

1. Distribute tributes to slang such as those quoted above and earlier in the text. Ask students to state in writing the extent of their agreement or disagreement and to support their opinions with examples.

2. Ask students to collect recent slang terms for topics that have generated an abundance of slang in the past: a good person, a bad person, a good car, a bad car, money, no money, failure, good or bad television programs, getting angry, losing a job, good or bad teachers. The exercise demonstrates to students the flexibility of language and prepares them for the innovations of poets.

3. You may wish to combine the teaching of slang with the teaching of euphemism and jargon. In all three categories standard English is avoided, but for different reasons.

For Dangerous Metaphors

Many examples of dangerous metaphors can be found in *Word Abuse: How the Words We Use, Use Us* by Donna W. Cross (Coward, McCann and Geoghegan, 1979).

1. An effective way to alert students to the dangers of metaphors and catchwords is to ask them to analyze the deceptive element found in nearly all proverbs. What are the exceptions that make many proverbs untrue? Proverbs do not have the subordinate clauses needed to put the proper qualifications on the main idea. Why not and what are the implications?

2. Any metaphor that is used extensively to sway public opinion should be scrutinized for oversimplification. At present, for example, there is much discussion of a nuclear freeze. The metaphor is effective in dramatizing an important problem, but is there a danger that it might blind us to the catastrophic dangers inherent in the many interrelated issues? Ask students to collect similar political, ecological, economic, or social metaphors from newspapers, news magazines, and television. Analyze these in class discussion or through written assignments.

2 Humor in Metaphor

When students understand the metaphorical elements in popular expressions, they are able to recognize the various kinds of humor that exploit hidden and senile metaphors. We have already seen how much the authors of traditional riddles relied on new metaphors when they entertained their listeners with witty comparisons. Today the situation seems to be reversed: a great deal of humor is created not by inventing new comparisons but by manipulating old ones, especially those that have lost most of their metaphorical vitality.

Metaphors Taken Literally

A surprising number of jokes and cartoons depend for their humor on our ability to recognize worn metaphors when they are taken literally. In one of its space fillers *The New Yorker* quoted the headline "Concorde Test Flights Could Land In Supreme Court," adding the comment, "Not without some remodeling." Mark Twain told customs officials that he had only clothing in his luggage; when the inspector found a bottle of bourbon, Twain replied, "That's my nightcap." Winston Churchill said that Stanley Baldwin occasionally stumbled over the truth but that he always picked himself up and hurried on as if nothing had happened. When an actor boasted that his performance was so impressive that he had the audience glued to their seats, Oliver Hereford replied, "Wonderful! Wonderful! Clever of you to think of it." Among the many cartoons in recent issues of *The New Yorker* are several that require metaphors to be taken literally. A native giving directions to an American tourist during a period of anti-American demonstrations says, "The U.S. embassy? It's just a stone's throw from here." A lawyer reading a client's will to the heirs seated in front of him announces, "To my nephew, Leroy Chittendon, who didn't know enough to come in out of the rain, I leave my umbrella." And a boss says to a napping subordinate, "Dammit, Donaldson, when I suggested you sleep on it, I didn't mean *here*."

We should note in this connection that recent scientific develop-ments have destroyed at least one popular metaphor. Ever since we

have had heart transplants the following metaphors have become
useless because they can all be taken literally: a change of heart, a
man after my own heart, and have a heart.

Perhaps the choicest humor involving metaphors taken literally is
found in Thurber's essay "The Secret Life of James Thurber." In
describing his boyhood, Thurber tells how often his private world
was enriched by expressions nonchalantly "tossed off by real-estate
dealers, great-aunts, clergymen, and such other prosaic persons."
When we look at the expressions that enchanted him, we find that
they are clichés, metaphors that were completely dead to the adults
who used them but very much alive to the child who heard them.
Although Thurber never uses the terms metaphor or cliché, he creates
his humor by recalling how as a child he took literally the dormant
metaphors in clichés. He recounts how his imagination was ignited
when he heard of businessmen

> who phoned their wives to say that they were tied up at the office,
> sat roped to their swivel chairs, and probably gagged, unable to
> move or speak, except somehow, miraculously, to telephone;
> hundreds of thousands of businessmen tied to their chairs in
> hundreds of thousands of offices in every city of my fantastic
> cosmos. An especially fine note about the binding of all the
> businessmen in all the cities was that whoever did it always did it
> around five o'clock in the afternoon.
>
> Then there was the man who left town under a cloud. Some-
> times I saw him all wrapped up in the cloud, and invisible, like a
> cat in a burlap sack. At other times it floated, about the size of a
> sofa, three or four feet above his head, following him wherever he
> went. One could think about the man under the cloud before
> going to sleep; the image of him wandering from town to town
> was a sure soporific . . . .
>
> I remember the grotesque creature that came to haunt my
> meditations when one evening my father said to my mother,
> "What did Mrs. Johnson say when you told her about Betty?" and
> my mother replied, "Oh, she was all ears." There were many
> other wonderful figures in the secret, surrealist landscapes of my
> youth: the old lady who was always up in the air, the husband
> who did not seem to be able to put his foot down, the man who
> lost his head during a fire . . . .
>
> I came into the house one rainy dusk and asked where Frances
> was. "She is," said our cook "up in the front room crying her
> heart out." The fact that a person could cry so hard that his heart
> would come out of his body, so perfectly shaped and glossy as a
> red velvet pincushion, was news to me. . . . My search for her
> heart took some fifteen minutes. I tore the bed apart and kicked
> up the rugs and even looked in the bureau drawers. It was no
> good. I looked out the window at the rain and the darkening sky.
> My cherished mental image of the man under the cloud began to
> grow dim and fade away. . . . Downstairs in the living room,
> Frances was still crying. I began to laugh.

The literal interpretation of a metaphor does not always produce humor. The Bible gives us one of the oldest examples of a communication problem created by such literalness. In John 3:1-7, Nicodemus must have the metaphor "born again" explained to him; he has taken it literally and asks, "How can a man be born when he is old? Can he enter the second time into his mother's womb, and be born?"

Metaphors Misunderstood

Metaphors that are not understood or are misunderstood can be the source of humor just as well as metaphors taken literally. A humorous passage in Henry Fielding's *Joseph Andrews* is based on the failure of a merchant to acknowledge that such words as *clothe* and *feed* can be used metaphorically. In chapter 17 of Book II, Parson Adams' host, a merchant, argues the superiority of his practical vocation because he provides the goods to feed and clothe clergymen and other impractical people. Parson Adams argues the superiority of the clergy: "Who clothes you with piety, meekness, humility, charity, patience, and all the other Christian virtues? Who feeds your souls with the milk of brotherly love, and diets them with all the dainty food of holiness, which at once cleanses them of all impure carnal affections, and fattens them with the truly rich spirit of grace? Who doth this?" The merchant replies, "I do not remember ever to have seen any such clothing, or such feeding. And so in the meantime, master, my service to you."

The metaphors of slang are probably the most often misunderstood and can be the source of frustration as well as of humor. In chapter 47 of *Roughing It,* Mark Twain says that the slang of Virginia City, Nevada, was "infinitely varied and copious" because every adventurer had brought with him the slang of his home community. This produced some difficulty in communication, as the following excerpt indicates. Scotty Briggs is calling on the new young minister to arrange for the funeral of Buck Fanshaw, and his metaphors create some problems:

> "Are you the duck that runs the gospel-mill next door?"
> "Am I the—pardon me, I believe I do not understand?"
> With another sigh and a half-sob, Scotty rejoined: "Why you see we are in a bit of trouble, and the boys thought maybe you would give us a lift, if we'd tackle you—that is, if I've got the rights of it and you are the head clerk of the doxology-works next door."
> "I am the shepherd in charge of the flock whose fold is next door."
> "The which?"

"The spiritual adviser of the little company of believers whose sanctuary adjoins these premises."

Scotty scratched his head, reflected a moment, and then said: "You ruther hold over me, pard. I reckon I can't call that hand. Ante and pass the buck."

"How? I beg pardon. What did I understand you to say?"

"Well, you've ruther got the bulge on me. Or maybe we've both got the bulge, somehow. You don't smoke me and I don't smoke you. You see, one of the boys has passed in his checks and we want to give him a good send-off, and so the thing I'm on now is to roust out somebody to jerk a little chin-music for us and waltz him through handsome."

"My friend, I seem to grow more and more bewildered. Your observations are wholly incomprehensible to me. Cannot you simplify them in some way? At first I thought perhaps I understood you, but I grope now. Would it not expedite matters if you restricted yourself to categorical statements of fact unencumbered with obstructing accumulations of metaphor and allegory?"

Blushing Metaphors

Not all the humor associated with metaphors is intentional. It happens all too frequently that metaphors that are seemingly dead or literal spring back to life when they are mistreated. Sleeping metaphors will be awakened and dead metaphors will twitch it they are placed in embarrassing company. Failure to recognize the latent metaphors in clichés and other literal terms can produce unintentional puns and other predicaments. A member of Parliament, criticizing unsanitary housing conditions and outdated facilities, observed that some houses "have sanitation unchanged since Queen Victoria sat on the throne." Some educators, apparently unaware of the metaphors of the drug culture, continue to urge giving our schools a shot in the arm so they won't go to pot. President Ford, defending his refusal to take sides in a congressional debate, remarked that he did not want to inject politics into a discussion of swine flu vaccine. The owner of a furniture store advertised, "We have a good reputation. We stand behind every bed we sell."

Mixed Metaphors

Mixed metaphors provide us with another source of unintentional humor. These expressions are so frequently misunderstood that we need to clear up some of the confusion surrounding them.

Mixed metaphors are not the same as expanded metaphors. Like Homer's similes, good metaphors can be developed through several stages without losing their effectiveness. Donne and other metaphysical poets often sustain through several stanzas the metaphors they derive from geography, navigation, astronomy, mathematics, religion, and gardening. Prose writers also provide many examples of successfully elaborated metaphors. Carlyle observed about Coleridge, "Never did I see such apparatus got ready for thinking, and so little thought. He mounts scaffolding, pulleys, and tackles, gathers all the tools in the neighbourhood with labour, with noise, demonstrations, precepts, and sets—three bricks." Hyde Cox and Edward Lathem devised a meteorologic comparison for Robert Frost in their introduction to *Selected Prose of Robert Frost* (Macmillan, 1968): "With a crowd he was ready (as a high-pressure area always is) to move into low-pressure areas. Like weather, he came in variously: sometimes suddenly like a storm, sometimes gently. But he seldom failed to change the climate when he moved in." One of our most beautiful expanded metaphors is also one of our oldest. When Edwin, King of Northumbria, tried to decide in 627 whether he should become a Christian, one of his councilors put the case for Christianity in this form: "So seems the life of man, Oh King, as a sparrow's flight through the hall when a man is sitting at meat in winter tide with the warm fire lighted at the hearth; but the chill rainstorm without. The sparrow flies in at one door and tarries for a moment in the light and heat of the hearth fire, and then flying forth from the other, vanishes into the wintry darkness whence it came. So tarries for a moment the life of man in our sight; but what is before we know not. What after it we know not. If this new teaching tell us aught certainly of these, let us follow it." Extended metaphors such as these are successful because in all the steps of their development the attention remains fixed on the basic concept being elucidated.

Mixed metaphors must also be distinguished from cumulative metaphors. Occasionally a writer will use a flood of metaphors to develop a point. The protagonist in *Cyrano de Bergerac* gets good results from this technique when he calls his nose a rock, a crag, a cape, a peninsula, a chimney, a chandelier, and a blue cucumber. In *Richard II,* John of Gaunt uses an accumulation of metaphors to declare his love for his native land:

> This royal throne of kings, this scepter'd isle,
> This earth of majesty, this seat of Mars,
> This other Eden, demi-paradise,
> This fortress built by Nature for herself
> Against infection and the hand of war,
> This happy breed of men, this little world,
> This precious stone set in the silver sea,

. . . .
This blessed plot, this earth, this realm, this England,
This nurse, this teeming womb of royal kings,

. . . .
This land of such dear souls, this dear dear land.

In "To a Skylark" and "Hymn to Intellectual Beauty" Shelley uses
a series of metaphoric similes in an analagous way. In the first stanza
of "To Autumn" Keats uses a succession of seven metaphoric infini-
tives to describe the richness generated by his opening metaphor, the
conspiracy between autumn and sun. These metaphors succeed because
they produce a unified effect.

Mixed metaphors, on the other hand, are logical absurdities. They
are combinations of two or more metaphors that smother whatever
sparks each metaphor might produce if allowed to stand alone. The
perpetrators of mixed metaphors do not respect the integrity or power
of a single metaphor, nor do they understand that if incompatible
metaphors are forced to coexist, the result will be confusion and
laughter.

One of President Nixon's science advisers reported that Nixon's
aides suspected scientists of using science as a sledgehammer to
sharpen their political axes. Used separately, the metaphors might
work: scientific knowledge misused might seem like a sledgehammer to
those victimized by it, and it could be made to forward one's political
ambitions. Crowding the two metaphors together, however, makes it
impossible for either to develop. Instead of being impressed with the
political power of scientists (the apparent intention of the metaphor),
we are left wondering how a sledgehammer might sharpen an axe.

A similar failure is apparent in the following mixed metaphors, all
of which managed in one way or another to find their way into print.

> It is unfortunate that it [Watergate] happened, but people are
> using it as a political football to bury my brother.—Donald Nixon
>
> I prefer the long distance runner to the short-term Band-Aid.
> —President Gerald Ford
>
> The noble lord shakes his head, and I am glad to hear it.
> —A British statesman
>
> I've heard a lot of insensitive debate in the House, but this rises to
> a new low—Quoted from the *Congressional Record* by *The New
> Yorker*, which added, "and sinks to a new zenith."
>
> A virgin forest is one in which the hand of man has not set foot.
> —A definition frequently reprinted
>
> I wouldn't be caught dead in that movie with a ten-foot pole.
> —An elderly woman in a Madison Avenue bus as it passed a
> theatre showing an x-rated movie

We still have many bottlenecks to iron out, so we'll have to touch all bases and play it by ear.—An anonymous politician, who may also have been an amateur musician

That snake in the grass is barking up the wrong tree.—A political candidate about his opponent

It may be significant that so many mixed metaphors come from politicians. Orators recognize the value of metaphors, and in the eagerness of politicians to express themselves as forcefully as possible they seem unable to stop with a single metaphor. However, the fact that most of their mixed metaphors are discordant clichés suggests that they are the products of lazy minds rather than minds searching for effective language. When Williard Wirtz was Secretary of Labor, he collected the following gems from Washington bureaucrats, reprinted on pages 179-80 in William and Mary Morris's *Dictionary of Word and Phrase Origins,* vol. 3 (Harper and Row, 1971).

You know, I've been keeping my ear to the grindstone lately, and I tell you we've got to do something to get a toehold in the public eye.

We're all going down the drain in a steamroller.

It's just a matter of whose ox is being goosed.

We can get this country out of the eight ball and make an honest man of J. Maynard Keynes in the boot. It may not work, but let's take a flying gambit at it.

We've got to be careful about getting too many cooks into this soup or somebody's going to think there's dirty work behind the crossroads.

Is it possible for mixed metaphors to succeed? Can a person switch from one metaphor to another without losing the effect of both? We have already noted that expanded and cumulative metaphors succeed because their separate parts have parallel meanings that contribute to a central purpose. In a mixed metaphor such a unified effect is almost impossible because its components, usually clichés, are so incongruous that jamming them together, often into a single phrase, produces dissonance rather than harmony. If the parts of a mixed metaphor are fresh, however, and if they are connected by strong feelings, they can be effective even if illogical. We do not object when Hamlet contemplates taking "arms against a sea of troubles" because the strength of his feelings transcends the contradictory metaphors. Neither do we object to Robert Lowell's vision of "spiders marching through the air, swimming from tree to tree" in his poem "Mr. Edwards and the Spider." Nor can we reject entirely the eloquence of Sir Boyle Roche, an Irish member of Parliament in the last quarter of the eighteenth century, whose political oratory produced some fascinating figurative formulations. Amusing as these expressions are, they convey a measure of his feelings, probably because they operate like successful paradoxes. These five examples are reprinted in Jeremy Lawrence's *Mix Me a Metaphor* (London: Gentry Books, 1972).

> My love for England and Ireland is so great, I would have the two sisters embrace like one brother.
>
> I stand prostrate at the feet of my Sovereign.
>
> The cup of Ireland's misfortunes has been overflowing for centuries, and it is not full yet.
>
> The profligacy of the times is such that little children, who can neither walk nor talk, may be seen running about the streets cursing their maker.
>
> Single misfortunes never come alone, and the greatest of all possible misfortunes is generally followed by a much greater.

Inert Metaphors

Mixed metaphors can be interesting failures because of the strength of the feelings involved. Inert metaphors are uninteresting failures because nothing happens; they are not clichés because they are new metaphors, but their newness is forced. The two terms brought together keep their distance. They do not like each other's company, so they refuse to embrace or even greet each other. If they are forced to coexist, they remain taciturn and often become sullen.

Robert Haldeman, one of President Nixon's aides, warned another aide about possible indiscretions, "Once the toothpaste is out of the tube, it's going to be hard to get it back in." This absurd comparison got the treatment it deserved from a reader of *Time*, who wrote, "Faced with this problem I've always unrolled the tube, cut the metal strip off at the bottom, squeezed the tube open, and replaced the toothpaste, and then rolled the tube back to its previous position. It's simple." Equally inert are some of the metaphors of country music: "My tears have washed 'I love you' from the blackboard of my heart"; "My heart has a mind of its own"; and "Drop-kick me, Jesus, through the goalposts of life."

The lesson to be learned from our observations about humor in metaphor—metaphors taken literally, metaphors misunderstood, and metaphors mixed and inert—is that our language is alive; it is alive because it is essentially metaphorical. Most words have a life of their own because they have acquired their meanings from metaphorical adventures. If we recognize that the metaphors in most of our popular expressions are dormant but not dead, we will not only avoid embarrassment but will learn to use language creatively. After all, the movement of words from literal to metaphorical to literal levels is a continuous cycle, something that sensitive writers can use to their advantage. Those who are not sensitive to this dynamic aspect of language are likely to have several problems with metaphors. Not only will they mix some and misunderstand others, they will also have a hard time recognizing when new metaphors fail.

Teaching Suggestions

1. Whether a metaphor succeeds or fails is not determined by objective standards; it is rather a personal, subjective judgment. Readers with comparable backgrounds would probably agree on the worth of most metaphors, but they might not agree on borderline ones, such as the following examples taken from a recent book on ecology, *The Fifth Horseman Is Riding* by Larry Van Goetham (Macmillan, 1974, pp. 1-6). Since these metaphors have obvious strengths and weaknesses, they can be used to study the difference between successful and unsuccessful metaphors. Do the terms interact or do they snub each other? If they interact, do they produce a unified result?

Example A

The history of our country is like a freight train that leaves the dawn of time with great wheels hauling hard to gain momentum. The train slowly gathers speed until it cruises, but the speed gradually builds up until the engine seems to surge with new and vast power, a juggernaut roaring on to crossroads that drift by so much faster than they did in earlier years.

Now the great engine seems to swell with power and it sucks fuel angrily. The train rides so fast that none of us can get off, and yet we are afraid to remain aboard because the train is riding pell-mell into darkness, where collisions are threatened at new crossroads. Now we have reached a tunnel whose end none of us can see. So many roads, so many decisions, and a dark road ahead. With the road so hard, is it strange that we should look back?

Example B

Yet still it haunts us—this image, the dream of America as it was, as we romanticize it from the vantage point, the fire tower as it were, of our century. It is a patent-medicine dream that has stuck in the minds of many Americans as if some huge camera obscura had clicked once, caught an image and fixed it for all times, a tintype of the young nation and its younger people.

2. Encourage students to speculate about the reasons for mixed metaphors. Are the authors of mixed metaphors groping for strong language or are they just piling up clichés for no good reason? Do not overanalyze mixed metaphors in these discussions; if students can laugh at them, they are learning some important principles of language.

Here are more examples that have appeared in print in recent years, most of them quoted in *The New Yorker*.

> If this idea ever catches fire, it will snowball across the land.
>
> Like a rare fish heavy with delicate roe, recording artist Willie Nelson has more music in the oven than a snow has rumors of falling.
>
> These sleek coaches should provide a tremendous shot in the arm to both legs of Nevada's passenger train system.
>
> It's not a good idea to sound like you're riding a losing horse and about to go down with the ship.
>
> This campaign is going to have a lot of twists and I think any reporter who tries to pigeonhole it is making a big mistake because there are too many wild cards.
>
> One-run baseball games always make great doorstops for the second guessers who love to throw open the gates and charge headlong into the land of 20-20 hindsight.
>
> This administration has an awful lot of other things in the pipeline, and this has more wiggle room so they just moved it down the totem pole.
>
> I think the proper approach is to go through this Garden of Gethsemane that we're in now, give birth to a budget that will come out of it, and then start putting our ducks in order with an appeal and the backup we would need to get something done at the state level.

3. For good measure and to use in conjuction with Willard Wirtz's collection given earlier, I list additional examples of government prose, gleaned mostly from daily newspapers. These might be called mixed clichés, expressions used by writers who demonstrate no sensitivity to the metaphorical element in our most common sayings. Students will enjoy these before they set out on a search for contributions of their own.

> He threw a cold shoulder on that idea.
>
> He deals out of both ends of his mouth.
>
> Let's do it and listen to how the shoe pinches.
>
> A study is underfoot.

He said it off the top of his cuff.

He got off on a sour foot.

It was a case of the tail biting the dog.

They were raking him over the ropes.

The problem started small, but it was baseballing.

4. Just as amusing as mixed clichés are mixed homonyms, absurd expressions made possible by careless listening, mispronunciation, and misspelling. The following contributions of federal employees are actually malapropisms, a term that comes from the character Mrs. Malaprop in Sheridan's *The Rivals*. She observed that her niece was as stubborn as an allegory on the banks of the Nile.

They treated him as if he had the blue bonnet plague.

He [an idealist] was a regular Don Coyote.

He has worked in several departments. He just put in a stench at HEW.

Going for the juggler again, eh, Art?

Don't flag dead horses.

It was a Fiat accompli.

5. Don and Alleen Pace Nilsen provide many interesting exercises on language and metaphor in their book *Language Play: An Introduction to Linguistics* (Newbury House, 1978).

3 Literal Comparisons and the Enticement of Metaphor

Before we proceed to the metaphors of poetry, we need to consider one further type of comparison. Having found metaphorical elements in riddles, folk expressions, clichés, slang, the literal definitions in a dictionary, and even in much contemporary humor, we have every reason to ask: "What, then, are literal comparisons, and how are they related to popular metaphors and to the metaphors of poetry?"

The comparisons that we encounter so frequently in daily affairs and in literature are literal if their primary purpose is to clarify by comparing something new with something familiar in as objective a fashion as possible. Each term of the comparison retains its literal dictionary definition, and there is no expectation that the terms will merge to form a new concept or to arouse strong feelings. Thus, when Mount St. Helens in the state of Washington erupted on May 18, 1980, reporters used literal comparisons to explain this new phenomenon in understandable terms. They said that the explosion produced a crater seven football fields long and three football fields deep. They said that the power of the explosion was equal to 500 of the bombs dropped on Hiroshima. The clarity of the second comparison depended on how well we remembered an earlier comparison, the statement by reporters in August, 1945, that the atomic bomb dropped on Hiroshima had the force of 20,000 conventional bombs. In most of their comparisons, however, reporters could not resist the enticement of metaphor, and they combined clarity with novelty and diversion: lava oozed from the bottom of the crater like bread dough, millions of trees were knocked down in rows as if a giant had been playing pick-up sticks, brown slime in the riverbeds looked as if someone had dropped an enormous chocolate ice-cream cone, Spirit Lake had become a cauldron of logs and boiling mud, the earthquake that shook the mountain caused it to blow its top just like the shaking of an unopened bottle of soda pop will cause the bottle to blow off its cap. When their comparisons took the form of personifications, the mountain awoke from its long slumber by first clearing its throat and then jiggling and dancing while releasing brief pulses of steam and ash; after it became spasmodic, it developed blisters of ice on its sides and sent up sullen plumes and pulsating clouds; when it tried to go back to sleep, it could doze only intermittently because it continued to belch and spit and spew and vomit.

Scientists understandably rely on literal comparisons to explain their research to the general public. A neuroscientist compared his research to removing a piece of transparent tape from a piece of glass; he had just begun to raise one corner of the tape and was fascinated by his discoveries. Another scientist wanted to emphasize that his latest discovery would speed up research in many fields: "It was as though we were standing in front of a library filled with millions of volumes we were unable to read. Now we can go inside and read to our heart's content." It is difficult to believe that scientists could explain their work without comparisons. Einstein, for example, had to use several concrete comparisons to explain his theory of relativity.

When Marilyn Horne explained how a mezzo-soprano must protect and cultivate her voice, she also made an interesting literal comparison: "Opera singers are very much like baseball players who can only pitch effectively every four or five days. We, too, can only sing effectively a couple of times each week. In between innings, a pitcher wears a jacket to keep his arm warm. When we're performing, we must also take care that our throat muscles don't get cold. In emergencies, when our vocal cords grow inflamed, we also get the same medical attention that pitchers resort to in order to cure a sore arm. Also, pitchers are very careful not to throw fast balls on every pitch in order to preserve their arm. Opera singers must also preserve their voices, and thus, cannot sing all out in every aria."

Literal comparisons are, of course, as essential in literature as anywhere else. In Book I of *Gulliver's Travels*, Swift faced the problem of explaining something totally unfamiliar to his readers. To describe what he saw in the world of the Lilliputians, he resorted to literal comparisons of necessity: buckets the size of a large thimble, a loaf of bread the size of a musket bullet, a lark smaller than a common fly, a crowd of brightly clad women like an embroidered petticoat spread on the ground.

In all of these literal comparisons, the similarity of things compared is obvious. The terms of the comparison are either from the same category (volcanic explosion and atomic explosion) or from categories that can be joined easily to provide the desired information. Those that might be called metaphors make more unpredictable comparisons (blisters of ice, the dances and spasms attributed to the volcano). Significantly, the literal comparisons often take the form of simile; by using a connecting word such as *like* or *as*, simile removes most of the uncertainty from a comparison and makes it as clear as possible. This does not mean, of course, that all similes are literal; those that use language in unconventional ways and compare elements that have little in common are in fact metaphors or, to be more precise, metaphorical similes. The presence or absence of the connecting word is a technicality and does not determine whether the comparison is literal or metaphorical. For the study of metaphor we will find it much more helpful to look at comparisons in terms of their emotional intensity rather than in terms of their structure, and to note that intensity is produced primarily by the degree of originality in the comparison and not by the presence or absence of *like* or *as*.

When a reporter wrote an article about a new supertanker, he noted that it was as long as the Empire State Building is tall and that it resembled a leviathan. Both comparisons are similes, but the first is literal because it transmits information objectively by bringing together two closely related terms of measurement. The second is metaphorical because it combines widely different categories to arouse emotion as well as to inform, conjuring up such ominous qualities as uncontrollable size and imminent destruction, qualities traditionally associated with the mythical sea monster. When a reviewer of a futuristic film called the robot in the film a cross between a hair drier and a mailbox, the comparison, though technically a metaphor because of the absence of *like* or *as*, would be literal to those who regard it as primarily descriptive but metaphorical to those who find it derisive as well as descriptive. When an astronaut tried to describe the precision required to launch a moon rocket, he remarked that finding the best approach to the moon was as difficult as finding a keyhole in the sky. This simile is probably metaphorical for most of us because it joins two disparate elements and produces more than a vivid description of a difficult task; the comparison also carries overtones of danger, perhaps even fear of failure.

Literature abounds with similes that must be considered metaphorical. In "What Fifty Said," Robert Frost comments about his early education, "I gave up fire for form till I was cold. / I suffered like a metal being cast." Technically, the first comparison is a metaphor and the second a simile, but both are clearly metaphorical because of the strength of feeling involved. In "On First Looking into Chapman's Homer," Keats uses three comparisons to describe the excitement of reading the new translation: his thrill was like that of a person traveling through realms of gold and finally reaching the richest realm of all, like that of an astronomer who discovers a new planet, like that of the explorers who were speechless when they saw the Pacific Ocean for the first time. In the first comparison Keats uses no connecting word and in the last two he does, which technically makes the first a metaphor and the other two similes. All three, however, are meta- phorical because they intensify as well as describe, they appeal to the imagination as well as to the intellect. The same holds true for the first simile in Wordsworth's sonnet "It Is a Beauteous Evening": the peaceful twilight scene on the beach is a holy time "quiet as a nun breathless with adoration."

We may conclude, then, that the primary function of literal com- parisons is to clarify; in most cases they are similes because they contain a connecting word that contributes to that clarity. Metaphori- cal comparisons are those that appeal to the imagination as well as to the intellect; sometimes they contain a connecting word, but more often they do not. Whatever their structure, their purpose is to make us feel as well as to understand. The foregoing examples show that literal and metaphorical comparisons often overlap; the difference between them is a matter of degree. In fact, purely literal comparisons are relatively rare outside the field of science.

As a final step in our approach to the metaphors of poetry, we need to reemphasize that both literal and metaphorical comparisons are indispensable. It is no exaggeration to say that comparisons are the basis for all growth and progress. Our very survival depends on our ability to integrate the new with the old by means of comparisons. We describe a new acquaintance by noting resemblances with people we already know. We describe a new song by comparing it with features of music already familiar to us. We learn the meaning of a new word by relating it to words we already know, and when we understand the new word we use it to define the next new word. We usually begin the study of a foreign language by defining its words in our native tongue, but as our vocabulary of foreign words grows, it in turn becomes the basis for definition. This cumulative process is essential to our growth. We can assimilate new experiences only if we can compare them with something we already know. When Jesus tried to explain his most revolutionary ideas, he relied extensively on comparison: "Whereunto shall I liken the kingdom of God," and "with what comparison shall we compare it?" Among his comparisons were a grain of mustard seed, a leaven, and a pearl of great price.

Shakespeare gives us a striking example of how frustrating a new experience can be when it cannot be related to the familiar. When Macbeth and Banquo meet the witches, Banquo cannot fit the witches into recognizable categories. They "look not like th' inhabitants o' th' earth, but yet are on't." They seem to understand his words, but for some time they speak no words of their own. They look like women, yet they have beards. He wonders whether they are projections of his fancy or whether they have outward form. When he asks them to look into his future as they already have into Macbeth's, they reply in paradoxes and remain enigmatic to him. He recovers his ability to see relationships, however, when he turns from the witches to Macbeth. He notices a change in Macbeth, but that change is within Banquo's range of experience, and he describes it with a comparison: "New honours come upon him, / Like our strange garments, cleave not to their mould / But with the aid of use."

Banquo's experience with the witches illustrates in a negative way the importance of recognizing relationships that make comparison possible. We cannot exist in a world of pure novelty. Endless repetition may bore us, but unrelieved novelty would be disastrous; it would disorient our lives and make survival impossible. We must maintain a balance between repetition and innovation; we require a basis for comparing the new with the old to make possible a merger of the two.

Although defining the new in terms of the old is an absolute necessity on the literal level, almost as essential are the more daring metaphorical comparisons designed to arouse feelings and stir people to action. When Martin Luther King campaigned against the segregation and exploitation of black Americans, he often climaxed his strongest arguments with vivid metaphors. In his famous speech at the Lincoln monument in August of 1963, he told the nation that Lincoln's Emancipation Proclamation "came as a great beacon light of hope to millions of Negro slaves who had been seared in the flames of withering injustice" but that one hundred years later "the life of the Negro is still sadly crippled by the manacles of segregation and the chains of discrimination." He called the Constitution and the Declaration of Independence "a promissory note" guaranteeing basic rights to all Americans, but went on to comment that the Negro people had found the note to be a bad check marked insufficient funds. He urged the nation to rise from "the quicksands of racial injustice to the solid rock of brotherhood." At the funeral of the four black children killed by a bomb while attending Sunday School in Birmingham in September, 1963, King said that their deaths should be a warning to "politicians who feed their constituents the stale bread of hatred and the spoiled meat of racism." When he accepted the Nobel Peace Prize in Oslo on December 10, 1964, he announced, "I refuse to accept the idea that mankind is so tragically bound to the starless midnight of racism and war that the bright daybreak of peace and brotherhood can never become a reality . . . that nation after nation must spiral down a militaristic stairway into the hell of thermonuclear destruction." For King the valley was a frequent metaphor for despair and the mountaintop a metaphor for hope. On April 3, 1968, the day before his death, he told an audience in Memphis that, like Moses, he had been to the mountaintop and seen the promised land.

Closely related to King's own metaphors are those of one of his biographers, Robert M. Bleineiss, who edited *Marching to Freedom: The Life of Martin Luther King, Jr.* (New American Library, Signet, 1969). Since this factual narrative has a dispassionate and objective tone, such metaphors as the following take on special meaning: "Memphis sat on the banks of the Mississippi River like a keg of dynamite over a spreading flame"; the protest in Albany in 1961 was a partial failure because the protestors did not have a "clear-cut target"; the preparations for the march on Washington in August, 1963, were, according to one federal official, like "getting ready for D Day in Normandy"; "hatred seeped through the nation that autumn [1963]. It was contagious . . . and it infected everything it touched."

These examples from Martin Luther King and one of his biographers show how powerfully metaphors dramatize serious issues. Writers and speakers looking for ways to counteract complacency turn frequently to bold metaphors to stimulate both thought and feeling.

Those seeking to entertain their readers and listeners also recognize the value of new metaphors. When sports communicators look for ways to enliven their descriptions, they utilize the full range of metaphor—from clichés to the bizarre to the poetic. Roger Angell, sports writer for *The New Yorker*, commented that Babe Ruth trotting out to left field resembled a "swollen ballet dancer with those delicate, almost feminine feet and ankles," that Thurman Munson was the center bearing and the jewel of the Yankee team, that Lou Brock was "narrow and sinewy, without a sag or a seam on him," that Nolan Ryan's fastball was a "liquid streak of white," that professional leagues expand like bubble gum, "ever larger and thinner." Vince Scully, sports announcer for the 1980 World Series, observed that Darrell Porter at the plate looks "like a man trying to swing a bat on the deck of a ship in a storm." Sportscaster Joe Garagiola said that Don Zimmer's face looked "like a blocked kick." When Al McGuire, experienced coach and sportscaster, previewed the NCAA basketball finals in March, 1981, his remarks included these:

> The most difficult coaching challenge this week will be getting the players off the clouds. A lot of coaches and players feel that they've accomplished something by breaking the sound barrier to get to the Final Four and forget that they have two more games to play.
> You have to retool real quickly and get that killer instinct. LSU's Dale Brown has to start climbing that mountain again. Indiana's Bobby Knight has to charge the machine-gun nest.

North Carolina's Dean Smith has to get that appointment as
chairman of the board. And Virginia's Terry Holland has to keep
trying to make them forget Thomas Jefferson in Charlottesville.

A few final examples from other fields conclude this demonstration
of our addiction to comparison. Charles Berlitz said that knowing
only one language is like living in a large house and never leaving
one room. When people were asking in the spring of 1981 why the
assassination attempts were directed at President Reagan and Pope
John Paul II rather than at lesser officials, a historian of violence in
American explained that assassins attack the highest ranking people
for the same reason that lightning hits the tallest trees. An economist
observed that successful taxation is the art of plucking the goose
without making it hiss. Ronald Reagan opened his acceptance speech
at the Republican National Convention in 1980 by saying it was
time to put the federal government on a diet. After he became president he said he would appoint federal inspectors who were as mean
as junkyard dogs. Reporters called Nancy Reagan an iron butterfly
and Rosalind Carter a steel magnolia. When Bob Straub was governor
of Oregon, he said that the bureaucratic paper work is like "yeast
in bread, foaming up over the top of the pan. The only way to control
it is to keep punching it down." A drama critic said that Katherine
Hepburn's voice was implacable as a dental drill. A London reporter
caused a minor international crisis when he said that Nancy Reagan
attending the royal wedding looked like John Wayne riding into
the sunset.

As F. L. Lucas acknowledged in an examination of style, "Why
such magic power should reside in simply saying, or implying, that A
is like B remains a little mysterious. . . . language often tends to lose
itself in clouds of vaporous abstractions, and simile or metaphor can
bring it back to concrete solidity; and, again, such imagery can gild
the gray flats of prose with sudden sun-glints of poetry" (*Holiday*,
March 1960, pp. 20–21). I would add to this statement the observation
that most comparisons seem to have a built-in metaphorical magnet
that draws them away from the literal realm. If we recognize this
feature in popular metaphors, we are prepared to examine the miracle
of poetic metaphors.

Teaching Suggestions

1. A visitor from England once commented that the headlines on
our sports pages were incomprehensible to him. Ask students to
imagine that they have a guest from another country to whom they

must explain the sports metaphors quoted earlier and those in such headlines and pronouncements as the following from *Track and Field News:* Nehemiah moves into the upper echelons of hurdlers; Nehemiah goes wild; Nehemiah still in the groove; Foster snaps a streak of five straight losses; Rono captures a real barnburner; Salazar hammered out laps in the 66–67 range, ignited the faithful, and caused crowds to yell their heads off; Scott puts mile out of sight; Salazar and Beardsley battle to the wire (it's a string, or a tape, not a wire, just as the boxing ring is actually a square); Salazar shadowed Beardsley, then surged ahead, outkicking his dogged pursuer; Grete Waitz dropped out of the marathon at 23 miles because her quadriceps locked up. The feature story on Dick Beardsley, second-place finisher in the Boston Marathon in 1982, was headlined, "The Man Who Pushed Salazar."

When Barbara Potter was asked why she progressed faster than some of her competitors in tennis, she replied, "I've waded through more muddy puddles." She also said, "When people say I'm an overnight success, I want to shred them" (*Sports Illustrated,* March 8, 1982).

Concerning the first NCAA track meet that combined men's and women's championships (Provo, Utah, June 1982) sportswriter Kenny Moore noted, "College women were in the meet for the first time, the NCAA having wooed and won them from the AIAAW by sheer animal magnetism—that is, money" (*Sports Illustrated,* July 16, 1982).

2. Books of quotations can be used as effectively as sports pages for assignments in finding metaphors to explain and analyze. Ask students to note how often the most memorable quotations are the ones with comparisons and that nearly always these comparisons are metaphorical rather than literal. Metaphors are most frequent in quotations that personify and elucidate such concepts as time, life, age, death, truth, beauty, speech, and words. Ask students to use books of quotations to list as many metaphorical comparisons as possible for an abstract concept such as *life*. They will find such comparisons as these: a game of dice, a pure flame, a theater, a school of gladiators, a shuttle, a mingled yarn, a dream, a tale told by an idiot, a jigsaw puzzle with most of the pieces missing, a one-way street, and an onion that cannot be peeled without crying. Similarly, *time* has been called a thief, a babbler, a river, a reaper, a whirligig, a nurse and breeder of all good, and a healer, while *words* are the physicians of a mind diseased, the soul's ambassadors, a cloud of winged snakes, and daggers, artillery, poniards, respectively.

A recent collection that deserves special mention is *The Quotable Women, 1800–1975,* edited by Elaine Partnow (Corwin Books, 1977). Here are a half dozen of the many metaphorical quotations found in this book:

> Now, as always, the most automated appliance in a household is the mother.—Beverly Jones

> Husbands are like fires. They go out when unattended.
> —Zsa Zsa Gabor

> I used to be Snow White . . . but I drifted.—Mae West

> People talk about love as though it were something you could give, like an armful of flowers.—Anne Morrow Lindberg

> Hollywood, the propaganda arm of the American Dream Machine.
> —Molly Haskell

> A man's home may seem to be his castle on the outside; inside, it is more often his nursery.—Clare Booth Luce

> Fear is a slinking cat I find / Beneath the lilacs of my mind.
> —Sophia Tunnell

3. Ask students to use examples from popular music to illustrate the ubiquity and necessity of metaphor. Songs are written not to be studied but to be understood the first time they are heard, a fact that rules out complex metaphors that might disrupt the pace of the song but does not rule out all metaphor. Even country music, which makes the least claim to literary sophistication, uses metaphor. One publisher of country music reportedly has said that some of the songs sent to him are so bad that he has to rewrite them before he can throw them into the wastebasket.

Whatever the quality of rock and country lyrics, the metaphors are there, mostly uninspired and obvious, but occasionally interesting and suggestive. A successful business man whose artificial values make him insensitive to human needs is said to have air-conditioned sinuses, eighty-six proof anesthetic crutches, and synthetic smiles. Those who are warned that they will not be exempt from the consequences of their actions are told that their gold-plated door will not keep out the Lord's burning rain. The elusive butterfly of love is chased with nets of wonder, the pursuer's footsteps echoing through the canyons of one's mind. Fidelity in love is equated with walking the line, keeping up one's end of the tie that binds, and being willing to give up one's "ownliness." The disappointed lover has learned to read between the pages of a look, to find love regarded as a transparent dream beneath an occasional sigh, and to find small things like reasons put into a jar. An alienated person imagines himself trapped in a mining disaster and asks Mr. Jones not to talk too loud lest he cause a landslide that would permanently entomb the speaker. To another alienated person the streets are uneven and faces come out of the rain. Another alienated person is tired of sitting on the sidetrack watching the main line run. The person who is too restless to marry has too many bridges to cross over, feels attracted to too many fields of tempting clover, and like the eagle is a prisoner of the wind. Some of the metaphors are synesthetic, transferring words from one of the physical senses to another: hungry eyes, green chilly winds, a vision softly creeping.

Students familiar with church music can find metaphors on just about any page of a hymnal.

4. Metaphors can be effective even when their meaning is not perfectly clear. Why has Julia Ward Howe's "Battle Hymn of the Republic" retained its enormous popularity ever since its composition in 1861? Abraham Lincoln was enthusiastic about it, and one scholar has said that the hymn helped the Northern cause more than trainloads of corn or ammunition would have done. It was sung at the funerals of Abraham Lincoln, Winston Churchill (at his request), and Robert Kennedy and at the inauguration of President Lyndon Johnson. In a speech in Memphis, Tennessee, the night before his death, Martin Luther King said: "I am happy tonight. I am not worried about anything. I am not fearing any man. Mine eyes have seen the glory of the coming of the Lord."

The hymn owes its popularity in part to the marching rhythm of the tune, used earlier for "John Brown's Body," and to the powerful expression of faith in the eventual triumph of right. But another reason for its popularity must be its vivid metaphors, especially those in the first stanza: "trampling out the vintage where the grapes of wrath are stored," "the fateful lightning of His terrible swift sword," and truth "marching on." Students will probably find these metaphors exciting even if they cannot explain them. When John Steinbeck wrote his publisher in 1938 that he had chosen *The Grapes of Wrath* as the title for his novel, he added, "I like the soft with the hard and the marching content and the American revolutionary content." He also suggested that the entire hymn be reprinted somewhere in the book.

5. Anything can be compared to anything else, often with fascinating results. Dramatize this point with unusual biblical comparisons presented as questions. I have included the answers, but you might want students to look up the metaphorical passages instead.

Comparisons from the Song of Solomon

Who is like

a locked garden, sealed fountain? (4:12, one's bride)

a mare of Pharaoh's chariot? (1:9, one's girlfriend)

What is like

a flock of goats moving down a hillside? (4:1, her hair)

a flock of shorn sheep that have come up from washing? (4:2, her teeth)

a scarlet thread? (4:3, her lips)

the halves of a pomegranate? (4:3, her cheeks)

the tower of David, built for an arsenal? (4:4, her neck)

the tower of Lebanon, overlooking Damascus? (7:4, her nose)

the best wine that goes down smoothly, gliding over lips and teeth? (7:9, her kisses)

doves beside springs of water? (5:12, a boyfriend's eyes)

alabaster columns set upon bases of gold? (5:15, his legs)

From the Book of Proverbs

Who is like

clouds and wind without rain? (25:14, a boastful person)

a ring of gold in a swine's snout? (11:22, a woman without discretion)

a broken tooth and a foot out of joint? (25:19, an unfaithful man in time of trouble)

a war club, a sword, or a sharp arrow? (25:18, a liar)

a continual dripping on a rainy day? (27:15, a contentious woman)

a merchant ship that brings food from afar? (31:14, a virtuous woman)

one who lies down in the midst of the sea or on the top of a mast? (23:34, a drunkard)

one who takes a dog by the ears? (26:17, a meddler)

a lovely hind, a graceful doe? (5:19, a young wife)

cold snow in time of harvest? (25:13, a reliable messenger)

one who spreads a net at your feet to trip you? (29:5, a flatterer)

a madman who throws firebrands, arrows, and death? (26:18-19, a liar) a broken-down city without walls? (25:28, a man without self-control)

a dog returning to his vomit? (26:11, a fool who repeats his foolishness)

What is like

apples of gold in pictures of silver? (25:11, a kind word)

a deep pit? (22:14, the mouth of a false woman)

an ox going to slaughter? (7:22, a foolish man listening to a loose woman)

the passing of a whirlwind? (10:25, the life of the wicked)

vinegar to the teeth and smoke to the eyes? (10:26, a lazy employee to his employer)

rottenness in one's bones? (12:14, an unfaithful wife)

wounds that go to the inner parts of the body? (18:8, words of a gossip)

a biting serpent and a stinging adder? (23:32, strong wine)

4 The Metaphors of Poetry

The metaphors of poetry share two important features with popular metaphors. Both have the same basic structure—merging two unrelated terms to form new images and concepts—and both have the same general purpose—providing new pleasures and new insights through unusual comparisons. But that is about as far as the similarities go. The essential differences between them will emerge as we identify the most important qualities of poetic metaphors.

Four Essential Qualities

An indispensable quality of poetic metaphors is that they are inseparable from their contexts. They are organic rather than ornamental. They are so thoroughly integrated with the meaning and form of a poem that they cannot be uprooted. Popular metaphors tend to be rootless; they can be passed around and reused. Poetic metaphors on the other hand are forever identified with their poems and authors and are therefore indestructible. They may appear in the title or first line of a poem and control the development of the thought and feeling, as in Robert Frost's "The Silken Tent," "The Road Not Taken," and "Desert Places" or in Emily Dickinson's "After great pain," "I taste a liquor never brewed," "There is no Frigate like a Book," and "I like to see it lap the Miles." They may appear at the end of a poem, where they help to unify and interpret the poem, as in Emily Dickinson's "A narrow Fellow in the Grass" and "A Bird Came down the Walk," in Matthew Arnold's "Dover Beach," and in Robert Lowell's "For the Union Dead." They may also appear elsewhere in the poem where they pull together several lines or stanzas and reverberate with meaning, as when Robert Frost says in "Two Tramps in Mud Time" that he likes to merge vocation and avocation "as my two eyes make one in sight."

A second quality of poetic metaphors is their freshness and uniqueness. If the reader of a poem is to get new pleasures and insights, poets obviously cannot rely on clichés. Newness is indeed the essence of poetic metaphors. It represents the poet's ability to transcend the dullness and restrictiveness of literal language. Poetic metaphors seldom lose their uniqueness because, as we have seen, they are inextricable from their contexts. Note, for example, that the following partial metaphors, though familiar to many readers, retain the vitality of the poems in which they occur: the fog coming on cat feet, two roads diverging in a yellow wood, a patient etherized upon a table, ignorant armies clashing by night, traveling in realms of gold, the twin legs of a compass, a tree planted by the river of waters, a tale told by an idiot. Even when a poetic metaphor enters the main stream of public discourse—there's something rotten in Denmark, for example—it retains its vitality in its original context.

A third quality of poetic metaphors is that their newness produces not only surprise but also tension. To produce surprise and tension, a poet has to take chances. As Lawrence Ferlinghetti says in his poem "Constantly Risking Absurdity," poets, like acrobats on a high wire, are capable of reaching new heights of beauty and reality, but they can also lose their balance and fall into absurdity. As Edward Lueders observes in "Your Poem, Man," poets have to experiment, to produce "surprise and wild connections," to "try untried circuitry," and to "tell it like it never was" so readers "can see it like it is."

The fourth quality of poetic metaphors is in some ways an extension of the third. The two terms being merged in a metaphor must interact in subtle and interesting ways. They must ignite each other but not completely destroy each other. This quality of creation through partial destruction is the most mysterious and the most appealing aspect of metaphor, as we can see in the following efforts of critics to explain it.

In *Metaphor and Reality* (Indiana University Press, 1962) Philip Wheelwright argues that a metaphor should be judged by "the quality of the transformation that is brought about." To what extent does it "intensify one's sense of reality"? What is "the psychic depth at which the things of this world, whether actual or fancied, are transmuted by the cool heat of the imagination"? "Cool heat," incidentally, is an interesting oxymoron, suggesting some of the paradoxes and mysteries at the heart of metaphor.

Winifred Nowottny points out in *The Language Poets Use* (Humanities Press [Athlone Press], 1962) that we must learn to distinguish between "metaphors in which the linking of extremes is ham-fisted and the result is boring or embarrassing, and metaphors in which the linking of extremes gives 'a sense of sudden liberation'; it depends on what sort of a 'complex' is presented, whether we are impressed or not."

In 1974 the editors of *New Literary History* devoted an entire issue to discussions of metaphor. In one article F. E. Sparshott noted that the "trick in metaphorical thinking is to superimpose two complex frames of reference and play them off against each other, to grasp at once the ways in which one thing is like another, to avoid altogether the ways in which one thing is damagingly unlike the other, but above all to let the mind play around the fringes where it can catch glimpses of remote and improbable likenesses." In another article James Deese observes that "the literal and figurative concept must have some features in common . . . but they had better be neither too numerous or salient." As he says, nothing is gained by calling a tiger a lion. Neither can a metaphor be "too obscure and dependent upon a kind of erudition" lest it be dismissed as "only a clever trick."

Owen Barfield says in his third edition of *Poetic Diction: A Study in Meaning* (Wesleyan University Press, 1973) that the extent of the comparison is the crux of metaphor. When a poet writes B but really means A, the relationship between B and A cannot be too obvious. "The difficult and elusive relation between A and B is the heart of any matter." The easier it is to be certain that B equals A, the worse the poem. We have to feel that expressing A as B is necessary, even inevitable, that B is "the best, if not the only way of expressing A satisfactorily. The mind should dwell on it as well as on A and thus the two should be somehow inevitably fused together in one meaning."

Tension, surprise, dynamic interaction of two nearly incompatible terms, interlocking of metaphor and context—these are the qualities mentioned most frequently by critics and scholars trying to describe successful poetic metaphors. Let us now find examples of these qualities in the works of a poet whose metaphors are unusually daring and provocative.

The Metaphors of Emily Dickinson

Emily Dickinson observed in "This was a Poet" that a poet must distill "amazing sense from ordinary Meanings"; this is exactly what she succeeds in doing when she creates her most fascinating metaphors. In "Bees are Black" she calls bees "Buccaneers of Buzz," a metaphor that contains most of the qualities discussed above. There is a moment of tension while we decide how to respond to the comparison of bees with pirates, but almost immediately unexpected similarities begin to emerge and the metaphor produces new insights and pleasures. We recognize several qualities of pirates that could be applied to bees: audacity, energy, mystery, stealth, excitement, courage. The similarities become so appealing that they cause us to ignore the many ways in which bees and pirates are not alike and invite us instead to concentrate on the overlapping area where the metaphor is produced.

Other examples of Dickinson's skill with metaphors are found in her treatment of some of the most commonplace images in literature, such as those relating to the sun. In "I'll tell you how the Sun rose" she describes the sun rising "a Ribbon at a time"; in the setting sun she sees the pageantry of yellow boys and girls climbing a stile and being led away. In "They called me to the window" the setting sun is a sapphire farm, a herd of cattle, and a sea filled with ships for which the mountains are the crew; in "I never told the buried gold" it is a pirate crouching low to guard the gold he has plundered during the day; in "She sweeps with many-colored Brooms" it is a bustling housewife with flying aprons who sweeps the skies with colorful brooms and litters earth and sky with "Purple Ravelling," "Amber thread," and "Duds of Emerald."

Emily Dickinson's skill with metaphor is also revealed in her ability to put the essence of an entire poem into a well-chosen metaphor, usually in the first or last line. In "After great pain" she describes the numbness and exhaustion following great suffering as a "formal feeling," a general metaphor that sets the tone and meaning of the more specific metaphors that follow: "stiff Heart," "Quartz contentment," "Hour of Lead"; nerves sitting "ceremonious, like Tombs," feet mechanically following a "Wooden way," and the "Chill—then Stupor" of a person freezing to death. A similar function of opening metaphors occurs in "I felt a Funeral," "I taste a liquor never brewed," "What Inn is this," "I know where wells grow," and "My Life had stood—a loaded Gun." When a strong metaphor appears at the end of a poem, it can provide both a logical and psychological climax to the preceding metaphors and multiply the emotional effect of the poem. "A narrow Fellow in the Grass" begins with twenty lines of superb description of the movements of a snake and concludes with a description of the speaker's feelings. The speaker's reaction is described first as "a tighter breathing" and then as "Zero at the Bone." In "I would not paint—a picture" she considers the responsibilities and privileges of artists and concludes with a metaphor referring to poems as "Bolts of Melody." In "A Bird came down the Walk" she describes the movements of the bird in metaphors based on the most minute observations. When the bird disdains the offer of a crumb and decides to go home, she says it moves softer than "Butterflies, off Banks of Noon" who "Leap, plashless as they swim." The concluding metaphors in these three Dickinson poems are so vivid that they almost seem to detach themselves from their poems, but they are, in fact, brilliant culminations of the poems, subtly consistent with their contexts. If they cannot be analyzed, they can be admired for their incomparable beauty and power, for the excitement they create about the possibilities of language.

The ability of metaphors to sharpen our senses and delight us with fresh comparisons impresses us in many other poems of Emily Dickinson as well. In "A Lady red" she describes the onset of spring in terms of "tidy Breezes with their brooms" sweeping the countryside to prepare it for the new flowers. In "Besides the Autumn poets sing" she describes the onset of winter in terms of the disappearance of autumn fragrances. In "Like Brooms of Steel" the sun sends out "Faint Deputies of Heat," and when winter arrives the street is swept by wind and snow "Like Brooms of Steel." In "It sifts from Leaded Sieves" the snow "powders all the Wood," fills "with Alabaster Wool the Wrinkles of the Road," makes the countryside resemble an "Unbroken Forehead from the East," wraps fence rails in fleece, and "Ruffles Wrists of Posts." In "The Robin for the Crumb" the bird expresses its gratitude with a "Silver Chronicle," and in "A Route of Evanescence" the hummingbird's flight is "A Resonance of Emerald— A Rush of Cochineal." In "Like rain it sounded" the rain "warbled in the Road," "pulled the spigot from the Hills," and then disappeared like Elijah "Upon a Wheel of Cloud." In "One joy of so much anguish" the birds that sing in the morning stab the speaker's ravished spirit with "Dirks of Melody."

The above is but a sample of Emily Dickinson's incredible achievement with metaphor. No one can be expected to admire all of these metaphors, but students should have no trouble finding interesting ones for discussion.

Four Kinds of Metaphor

Teaching in some detail the metaphors of a single author is an effective tactic, but it should be supplemented by at least one more approach. We can enhance our teaching of metaphor considerably if we emphasize that good metaphors need not be obscure, that there are many degrees of difficulty among good metaphors. One way to teach this important fact is to arrange selected metaphors in terms of complexity, perhaps using a fourfold classification.

1. *Casual metaphors,* those that we tend to take for granted until their metaphorical qualities are pointed out to us, those that Robert Frost called grace metaphors. This category would not include clichés

and other worn metaphors, but it would include a large number of synesthetic metaphors, those that interchange the terms that apply to the various senses: sight (visual), sound (auditory), smell (olfactory), taste (gustatory), touch (tactile), and tension and movement (kinesthetic). The person who described architecture as "frozen music" created a metaphor by combining a tactile term (frozen) with an auditory term (music) to define a visual concept (architecture). Milton mixed visual and gustatory terms when he denounced mercenary clergymen as "blind mouths." Sounds are often animated with visual descriptions: Euripides' "the trumpet call flashed out like a beacon," Blake's "hapless Soldier's sigh" that "runs in blood down Palace walls," Keats's "scarlet pain," "purple riot," "silent form," and "argent revelry." Classical music is often described as warm or cold, soft or hard, heavy or light. During the intermission of a televised performance of an opera, a distinguished musician commented that each opera has its own "smell, taste, and color." Popular musicians use such terms as "hungry eyes," "listen to the warm," and "a flash of neon touched the sounds of silence." Among our popular sayings are such metaphors as "I have a dark brown taste in my mouth" and "Don't look at me in that tone of voice." All of these are elementary metaphors, even if we apply the somewhat pretentious word *synesthetic* to them (metaphors of mixed senses might be an alternative). We may not give much thought to the way we interchange the language of the senses, but every time we do it we create a metaphor, sometimes a very delightful one, as when Nabokov said that occasionally he liked a "triangular gulp of beer."

2. *Sensuous metaphors,* those that we enjoy primarily for their strong, original images. Usually we enjoy their precision and clarity, sometimes their ambiguity. They are primarily descriptive and do not inspire much thought; if we do pause over them, it is to relish their novelty and beauty.

Elizabeth Bishop in her poem "The Map" describes a peninsula as taking "the water between thumb and finger like women feeling for the smoothness of yard goods" and refers to the coastline as profiles that "investigate the sea." In "Silence" Marianne Moore refers to a cat carrying off a mouse with its "limp tail hanging like a shoelace from its mouth." Robert Lowell in "Skunk Hour" refers to a "mother skunk with her column of kittens." Robert Frost in "Mowing" tells about his "long scythe whispering to the ground." In *Sometimes a Great Notion* Ken Kesey refers to "clouds grinding against the mountains," the "sucking hiss of wet tires," and hounds that came "pouring" and "boiling" from under the porch. A feature in *Reader's Digest,*

Picturesque Speech, has printed such metaphors as these: "hail type-writing on the roof," "a spider rappelling from the ceiling," "elephants vacuuming the earth," "percolators doing push-ups," "flames snapping their fingers in the fireplace," and "shirts cheerleading on the clothesline."

3. *Resonant metaphors,* those that add implication to sensuousness. While it is true that all metaphors suggest more than literal meanings, we can usefully limit the term to those metaphors that inspire thought as well as feeling. We grasp them fairly quickly, but we are also held for a moment by their implications.

Stephen Spender in his poem "An Elementary Classroom in the Slum" describes undernourished children as wearing "skins peeped through by bones." He says that teachers should encourage children to "let their tongues run naked into books." In "What I Expected" he sees "cripples pass with limbs shaped like questions." Theodore Roethke begins his elegy "Death Piece" with the metaphor "invention sleeps within a skull."

4. *Complex and subtle metaphors,* those that require us to reflect to get even a fraction of their multiple meanings. The comparisons are not as specific or as obvious as those in the first three groups. In fact, comparisons are now of less interest than the sheer force and richness of the final impression.

When Spender in "An Elementary Classroom in the Slum" describes one of the school children as "the stunted, unlucky heir of twisted bones, reciting a father's gnarled disease," he packs enormous social and educational pathos as well as personal tragedy into a single metaphor. Robert Lowell in "For the Union Dead" observes that the aquarium has been replaced by "giant finned cars"; he concludes with a metaphor that brings to a magnificent climax his lament over the materialism in old South Boston: "a savage servility slides by on grease." Nelly Sachs, German-born Jewish poet and playwright who won the Nobel Prize for literature in 1966, barely escaped confinement in a concentration camp by fleeing to Sweden in 1940. "Writing is my mute outcry," she has said, a comparison suggested by one of the metaphors in her "Chor der unsichtbaren Dinge" (Chorus of Things Invisible): "Wailing wall night / Carved in you are the psalms of silence." Even in translation, this metaphor expresses depths of feeling that simply cannot be paraphrased.

5 Identifying Symbols and Distinguishing Them from Metaphor

Symbols and metaphors share several qualities, but they are far from being synonymous. Both are figurative expressions that transcend literal language. Both rely heavily on implication and suggestion. Both present the abstract in concrete terms, and both can be interpreted with varying degrees of openness or specificity. They differ, however, in important ways. A symbol expands language by substitution, a metaphor by comparison and interaction. A symbol does not ask a reader to merge two concepts but rather to let one thing suggest another. A symbol derives its meaning through development and consensus, a metaphor through invention and originality. A symbol is strengthened by repetition, but a metaphor is destroyed by it.[1]

The terms *symbol* and *sign* are often used interchangeably in popular discourse. Most dictionaries, for example, have a supplementary section called "Arbitrary Signs and Symbols" in which are listed standardized signs in mathematics, in finance, and in many other fields. These graphic devices illustrate two basic qualities of signs: their meaning is arbitrary and they stand for only one thing. Signs are the dozens of signals to which we respond routinely every day—colors, gestures, shapes, patterns, motions, sounds, tones—whatever we experience through our senses and recognize both for what it is in itself and the other thing it represents. When we hear a siren, we comprehend both the shrill sound and the meaning we have given it—a fire truck, an ambulance, a police car, an approaching air raid, the all-clear after an air raid. Because we have codified the meanings of our signs, we repond to them instantly and consistently with a minimum of thought.

The most important signs in our lives are, of course, words themselves. Written words are only trails of ink and spoken words are only disturbances of air waves that we have made into signs by giving them arbitrary meanings. To facilitate our use of these signs, we have placed them in dictionaries lest we forget their designated meanings. However, as we have noted in our discussion of literal words, a dictionary is not a prison, and words keep breaking away from whatever literal restraints we place on them.

A word advances from a sign to a symbol when it is used to elicit extended thought and feeling rather than an automatic response. The literal meaning is not destroyed, but it is used in such a way that we suspect that it stands for something else. Thus water is used symbolically so often that whenever we come across the word in literature we consider the possiblility that it symbolizes purity and holiness or, in ironic contexts, the opposite.

Learning to recognize symbols is largely a matter of using our intuition and our background in literature. We should remember first of all that anything may be a symbol, that a symbol is any sign that has acquired extra meaning. It may be an object, a gesture, an incident, a person, a plot, a color, a sound, a pattern or sequence of action—anything that reminds us of something else that in turn seems applicable to the text before us. The word *may* is crucial. Although we must develop a sensitivity to the possibility that anything unusual *may* be symbolic, we must refrain from concluding that everything unusual *is* symbolic. A balance between sensitivity to the possibility of symbols and a commonsense approach to the basic meaning of the text is the best guide. With this warning before us, we are ready to consider some of the best ways of identifying symbols.

Repetition

Since good writers do not resort to padding, we can assume that whatever is repeated must be significant and may be symbolic.[2] In Bernard Malamud's short story "A Summer's Reading," Catanzara is called a changemaker, a term that acquires significance from the number of times it is repeated. The term is first of all literal; Catanzara earns his living working in the change booth of the city transportation system. But as the story develops, the term becomes humorously symbolic. Catanzara has failed to change his own life and is trying to assume the role of changemaker in the life of the central character, George Stoyonovich. Another instance of repetition in the story is also symbolic. Whenever Catanzara reads the *New York Times,* his unattractive wife hovers over him from an overhead window. We might assume that reading the *Times* symbolizes aspiration or achievement, but in this story the symbol suggests frustration, compromise, and defeat—an action symbolic of Catanzara's inability to rise above his dreary life. In Indro Montanelli's short story "His Excellency," a major symbol is also established through repetition. The central character disguises his criminal past by posing as a distinguished general.

The symbol that defines his role playing in several crucial scenes is his monocle, a constant reminder that he is an impostor. In Irwin Shaw's short story "An Act of Faith," the Luger receives much attention and becomes the symbol for the main character's conflict between faith and fear.

Connotation

Since all symbols have rich connotations, the question arises whether all connotations are symbolic. In a sense they are since they suggest meanings that go beyond the literal level. Even though the terms overlap a bit, we can make a useful distinction: *connotation* is the more general term for the extra meanings that some words have acquired, and *symbol* is the more specific term for the words and techniques that have fairly definite extra meanings. Thus a word like *denial* probably has fairly vague negative connotations for most of us, but if that quality is represented by the crowing of a cock or by a negation repeated three times we call the representation a symbol; as readers we are expected to recognize the implicit reference to Peter's denial in the New Testament and to use it to add meaning to the immediate text. Similarly, the word *betrayal* has negative connotations of a general sort, but if the idea is expressed by thirty pieces of silver, by throwing reward money to the ground (as in Prosper Mérimée's story "Mateo Falcone"), or by the name *Judas* (as in Katherine Anne Porter's "Flowering Judas," in Frank O'Connor's "Judas," and in John Brunner's science fiction story "Judas"), we are dealing with symbols; the story of Judas in the New Testament is intended to enrich the meanings of the stories at hand.

Allusion

All allusions should be regarded as symbols or metaphors or both. If the parallels between an allusion and a text are fairly numerous, the allusion is metaphorical because it invites the making of comparisons. Most allusions, however, function like symbols because they transfer extra meanings and emotions from an earlier source to the text at hand without making comparisons. The most important question about an allusion is not whether it is a symbol or a metaphor (often it is both), but how it is used. Allusions, whether symbols or metaphors, can function in a variety of ways.

To Children's Literature

In the poetry of the last two decades, allusions to children's literature have become frequent, diverse, and significant. These allusions can be considered under three headings: the image of women, social protest, and the search for meaning.

The Image of Women

Some of the most intriguing allusions to children's literature are found in poems that reverse the traditional image of women. In these poems familiar stereotypes are turned into symbols with new meanings. In Naomi Lowinski's shaped poem "Rapunzel" (*Berkeley Poets Cooperative,* no. 4, 1972), the princess contemplates cutting her hair and leaving the tower not as a princess, "a body waiting for a lover," but as her own person—a "somebody." In "Bedtime Story" (*The Poetry Review* 60 (1969): 49), Cecily Taylor challenges the traditional assumptions in several familiar children's stories. The frog-prince, the princess's dancing slippers, the pea and the mattress, the ugly duckling, the golden goose, the straw and the spinning wheel, are woven into a mother's bedtime story that concludes:

> Sleep well, my children,
> and tomorrow night,
> if I am not here,
> Daddy will tell you
> how the Princess
> escaped from the tower.

In Nina Nyhart's "The Pumpkin Eater" (*APHRA: The Feminist Literary Magazine,* Winter 1970), Peter is ridiculed for the pumpkin-shell world into which he put his wife—"round and orange" with "tame islands"—and for the naive chauvinism behind his question, "Why does she ask for a boat, a door?" An interesting reversal also occurs in A. D. Hope's "Coup dê Grace" (in his *Collected Poems,* Viking, 1972). Just when the wolf with "shag jaws and slavering grin" steps from the wood and "opens to gobble" Little Red Riding Hood, she opens her "minikin mouth" (complete with milk-teeth and pink tongue) and swallows him: "O, what a lady-like trick!"

Social Protest

Several poets allude to children's literature in making social protests of various kinds. In "Counting the Mad" (in *Contemporary American Poetry,* ed. Donald Hall, Penquin, 1962), Donald Justice converts the nursery rhyme "This Little Piggy Went to Market" into a symbol of the mistreatment of mental patients—and by extension our failure to understand all sensitive people:

> This one was put in a jacket,
> This one was sent home;
> . . . .
> And this one cried No No No No
> All day long.

In her sonnet "The Builders" (*Saturday Review*, November 25, 1961), Sara Henderson Hay takes her symbols from "The Three Little Pigs." The third pig represents those who would absolve themselves from responsibility for the deaths of those they might have saved:

> I told them a thousand times if I told them once:
> Stop fooling around, I said, with straw and sticks.

His attempt to rationalize his guilt ("Well, what is done is done.") appropriately conveys another literary allusion, this one to the attempt of Lady Macbeth to quiet her conscience and that of her husband after their murder of Duncan. In "Jack and the Beanstalk" (*The Antioch Review*, Summer 1961), Patricia Goedicke uses Jack climbing to "the furthest peak of his own ridiculously blooming green mystery" as a symbol for the wholesome curiosity so badly needed in our complacent society. In "Oh Baby Bear" (in *Contemporary Women Poets*, ed. Jennifer McDowell, Merlin Press, 1977), Ann Katz uses Goldilocks as a symbol for the kind of fulfillment denied modern women:

> Unlike Goldilocks and the beds,
> where will we ever be satisfied?

The Search for Meaning

Several poets have turned to children's literature to dramatize their search for meaning in life, finding in that literature symbols for renewal, for integrity, for innocence, for happiness, for simplicity, for unity, for alternatives to personal wastelands. In "Reading the Brothers Grimm to Jenny" (*The New Yorker*, November 4, 1967), Lisel Mueller wonders whether she should continue to offer her child the unreal and false world of fairy tales: "Why do I read you tales in which birds speak the truth . . . ?" She concludes that she must because as she preserves the imaginative world of the child she reminds herself of what her own world might be:

> And what can I, but see
> beyond the world that is,
> when, faithful, you insist
> I have the golden key—

In Robert Wallace's "Saturday Movie" (in his *Views from a Ferris Wheel*, Dutton, 1965), the child's fascination with the fairy tale enacted on the screen causes the father ("an aging prince with innocence on his arm") to mourn the disappearance of magic from his life. In Jill King's "A Child's Answers" (*Atlantic*, July 1967), the adult speaker envies the faith of a child that the drouth will end and that the fe-fi-fo-fumming giant sun who has "gulped up the dam and gobbled down the crops" will eventually be destroyed. The child is not surprised when the rains come because the child lives in a world where all ogres are doomed and all problems have solutions:

> Because this was the end foretold though the grown-ups doubted,
> this was the doom of ogres.

To Classical and Biblical Literature

Classical literature is probably the most frequent and the most familiar source for allusions, and two contemporary poems illustrate very different ways of using classical allusions symbolically. In Alastair Reid's "Daedalus" (*The New Yorker*, March 11, 1967), the only reference to Greek literature is the title, yet the entire poem is enriched by the parallel. The father in the poem admires the Icarian qualities of his small child ("My son has birds in his head."), debates with himself whether he should warn the child about the dangers of the future ("Am I to call him down, to give him / a grounding, teach him gravity?"), and then, unlike the classical Daedalus, decides to let the child explore the sky and enjoy his freedom ("Time tells us what we weigh, and soon enough / Age, like a cage, will enclose him."). The allusion, though mentioned only once, is pervasive.

In George Cuomo's "A Passing Helper Was His Father" (*Saturday Review*, March 30, 1963), the classical allusion appears inconspicuously at the end of the poem, but it too deepens the meaning of the entire poem. The poem, inspired by a news story about a father who directed traffic at the scene of a fatal accident for several minutes before he realized that it was his son who had been killed, treats an emotional episode with restraint but comes to a climax in the subtle allusion to another tragic father-son encounter, the one in which Oedipus unknowingly killed his father. In both instances father and son were brought "deadly together and unknown, / At some dark spot where two roads meet." The allusion links the poem to a memorable event in dramatic literature and serves as an effective conclusion to a poem rich in pathos but spare in words.

Biblical allusion, like allusions to classical literature, are a rich and powerful resource. In *The Scarlet Letter*, Hawthorne's allusions to the Bible clarify and intensify the suffering of Hester, the hypocrisy of Dimmesdale, and the heartless self-righteousness of the Puritans. Other allusions suggest that Hester and Pearl may fulfill a redemptive function in this stern society. In *Billy Budd,* Melville's allusions to the Bible emphasize the importance and complexity of the questions about the nature of evil and its relation to goodness and innocence. In *Cry, the Beloved Country,* Alan Paton's biblical allusions set the basic pattern of the story and ennoble the actions and feelings of the central character, Stephen Kumalo. In Steinbeck's *The Pearl* and in Kurt Vonnegut's *Slaughterhouse Five,* biblical allusions are used ironically to develop both theme and character. In "By the Waters of Babylon," Stephen Vincent Benét's biblical allusions create an apprehensive mood and cast a pall over the story as a whole, all of which help the reader experience the destruction of American civilization much more deeply. For extended discussion of these and many other biblical allusions, see Roland Bartel, James Ackerman, and Thayer Warshaw, *Biblical Images in Literature* (Abingdon Press, 1975).

The example of thirty pieces of silver referred to earlier reminds us that certain numbers serve as symbols, particularly numbers with well-known associations with the Bible, in mythology, and in folklore. When we encounter these numbers in literature we cannot automatically assume that they are symbolic allusions, but we should consider that possibility. The number three, for example, can refer to the trinity, to the three temptations of Jesus, to the three denials of Peter, to the three victims on the cross, to the three days between the crucifixion and the resurrection, to the three Hebrew children in the fiery furnace, to the three sons of Noah, to the three comforters of Job, to the three days Jonah spent in the belly of a whale, to the three fates of classical mythology, and on and on. The number six can refer to the six days of creation in Genesis, and seven to the day of rest. The number ten might refer to the ten commandments, the ten plagues of Egypt, the ten lepers who were cleansed, the ten children of Job (especially if seven sons and three daughters are specified). Twelve can refer to the labors of Heracles, the age of Jesus when he visited the temple, the twelve disciples, the twelve sons of Jacob, and the twelve tribes of Israel. The number thirty-three, the age at which Jesus died, has become quite firmly established as a symbolic allusion to Jesus while the number forty can refer to Jesus' forty days in the wilderness or to the forty years the Israelites spent on the way from Egypt to Canaan. All these numbers are used discursively much more frequently than symbolically, but when they appear in literature we must at least consider the possibility that they are symbols. In his poem "The Horses," Edwin Muir refers to "the seven days war that put the world to sleep," an ironic allusion that effectively juxtaposes destruction and creation. When Wallace Stevens says in "The Death of a Soldier" that the slain soldier "does not become a three-days personage," the allusion to the resurrection becomes a symbol for what the soldier lacks: he is not a Christ-figure, he will not rise from the dead, his death will receive little notice. In folklore many numbers have acquired special auras, but it is only the number thirteen that has become a consistent symbol.

Flexibility and Diversity

The meaning of symbols can be altered, even reversed, by cultural circumstances. In older Oriental and Indian cultures the swastika was a symbol of good luck, but Nazi Germany has probably converted it permanently into a symbol of tyranny. Before World War II, China was used as a romantic symbol in the love song "Slow Boat to China," but with the emergence of Red China, the song disappeared. Will it be revived by our changing attitudes toward China, or has the disappearance of slow boats doomed the song forever? The great speckled bird is another example of a symbol that has been adapted to many purposes. In the Bible (Jeremiah 12:9) it is a symbol of a persecuted minority, which is also the meaning implied in the title of Jerzy Kosinski's novel *The Painted Bird*. In country music the great speckled bird has become a symbol of salvation and of the chosen remnant. Other recent uses suggest that the symbol owes its popularity to its glittering image more than to its biblical meaning: it has served as the name of an underground newspaper, a Canadian rock music group, and an album of rock music. Colors can also prove to be versatile symbols. Scarlet as used in the Bible can signify sin (Isaiah 1:18), or prosperity (II Samuel 1:24 and Proverbs 31:21-22), or royalty (Daniel 5:6-7). Hawthorne's use of the color in *The Scarlet Letter* may thus have more than one meaning.

To illustrate the point that symbols are not static, that their flexibility and diversity are important resources for writers, let us consider in some detail the symbols in John Millington Synge's one-act play *Riders to the Sea* and in Negro spirituals.

In Synge's Play

When *Riders to the Sea* opens, Cathleen finishes kneading a cake and begins to spin at the wheel; her movements suggest that a life-supporting activity has been replaced by an activity associated with the three fates and with death. The first reference to Maurya tells us that she is lying down (life is defeating her). The wind blows open the door (the natural elements are invading and destroying Maurya's family). Bartley makes a halter of the rope intended for Michael's burial (Bartley's fate begins to be identified with that of Michael). Maurya and Bartley talk past each other, not answering each other's questions, and we are aware of Maurya's helplessness in preventing her last son's fatal venture. Bartley puts on Michael's shirt (further entwining his fate with Michael's). When Maurya is reminded that she did not give Bartley her blessing, she aimlessly rakes the fire, accidentally removing the turf from the cake (in her confusion she neglects a primary duty toward her son and interferes with a life-giving process). Maurya walks with Michael's stick (as she explains, the usual sequence of life is reversed when the old depend on the things left them by the death of the young). Maurya takes bread to the spring well for Bartley, but she chokes when she tries to bless him and returns home with the bread (her inability to deal with her premonition that her last surviving son is headed for death; the futility of trying to delay death with the symbols of life and communion—bread and water). The dripping sails leave a track to the door (the encroachment of the sea upon Maurya's family). The women who arrive before the arrival of Bartley's body silently take their places and begin to keen (they have done this so often that the act has become a ritual). The white boards intended for Michael's coffin are used for Bartley's (the incident symbolizes the continuity of death in this doomed family). Maurya forgot to buy the nails for the coffin (subconsciously she may be trying to resist the crucifixion of her last two sons; her lapse of memory also indicates her mental state). The cocks crowed when the rowers found Michael's body (betrayal by the sea). Maurya recalls holding the baby Bartley on her knees when the body of Patch was brought in (foreshadowing). The gray pony (death) knocks the red pony (life) and Bartley into the sea. Maurya sprinkles holy water on Bartley and says the prayers herself (the young priest was wrong in his optimistic statements earlier in the play and is not at hand for the last rites; even in religious matters Maurya is abandoned). When the cup of holy water is empty, Maurya turns it upside down and places it on the table (she has done all she can and the end is near). The title, taken from the song of Moses celebrating the drowning of the forces of Pharaoh in the Red Sea, is an allusion that works like a symbol: the fate of Pharaoh's horsemen suggests the fate of the seafaring men in Maurya's family. Maurya herself stands as a symbol for those who have been forced by fate to face life with an attitude of resignation and acquiescence.

The color symbolism in the play is somewhat ambiguous and needs to be interpreted cautiously. Red is not always a symbol for life nor gray for death, but those are the meanings that work best in the report of Bartley's death. But red does not symbolize life when Maurya recalls that the body of Patch was brought in on a red sail. Black is the color most frequently mentioned; the pig with the black feet, the black night, the black cliffs of the north, the black knot on Michael's clothes, and the black hags keening Michael. If the color does not seem to be used symbolically, its connotations certainly strengthen the ominous tone. The white boards are a complex symbol. They are associated with Maurya's desire to give Michael a clean burial, but they also stand for death and the continuity of death in this family.

The flexibility of symbols is an important resource for writers and for readers, making possible multiple meanings as well as irony. Water, usually a symbol of rebirth and renewal, becomes an ironic symbol when it fails to perform this function, as in Synge's play and in Chekhov's short story "Gooseberries." The journey, one of the most persistent and consistent symbols of change and fulfillment, has a striking effect when it becomes a symbol of futility, as it does in this play and in John Steinbeck's novel *The Pearl*.

In Negro Spirituals

The importance of flexibility in the use of symbols is bountifully illustrated in Negro spirituals that derive their primary symbols from the Bible. Slave-singers desperately needed strong symbols to express their longing for freedom and a better life, and they found these symbols in the Bible. They adapted biblical stories to their purpose by stripping away everything but the central image or character. The narrative disappeared as did all description and ceremonial details, leaving only the core of the original, which could serve as a symbol in a variety of songs. Take, for example, the many spirituals about Jacob's ladder. The interesting story leading up to Jacob's dream and Jacob's interpretation of his dream are never mentioned, and in only one or two versions are the angels mentioned. In the best-known version of the song, Jacob's ladder is taken out of context and made into a symbol of aspiration, the never-ending struggle for self-improvement and progress. This symbol is left open so that it can mean both the struggle for self-respect and spiritual bliss as well as the struggle for freedom.

The same principle of symbolic adaptation applies to many other biblical spirituals. "Swing Low, Sweet Chariot" must be based on the story of Elijah's ascent into heaven, the only instance of an airborne chariot in the Bible, but the story itself and even the name of Elijah have disappeared, leaving the chariot to serve as a symbol of various kinds of release and rescue. The spirituals about Daniel in the den of lions concentrate on Daniel's miraculous protection and release, a symbol filled with intense meaning for an enslaved people, as is the closely related symbol of the survival of the Hebrew children in the fiery furnace (the three children are never named).

This basic aspect of literature, that an open symbol cannot be restricted to the original context from which it draws its primary meaning, operates just as effectively in the songs that retell parts of the original story. David's slaying of Goliath, Joshua's destruction of Jericho, Gideon's defeat of the Midianites, Lazarus' elevation over Dives, and most important of all, Moses' emancipation of the Israelites—all these stories of victory in the face of overwhelming odds contained profound symbolic implications for the slaves.

One biblical symbol, the Jordan river, provides a good example of the many meanings a symbol can acquire. The river is shallow, meandering, and muddy. It has not been celebrated for its beauty or its utility as have such rivers as the Danube, the Rhine, the Volga, and the Mississippi. And yet, the mere mention of the name of the river arouses stronger emotions than the name of any other river, probably because of its symbolic function in spirituals.

Although the Jordan River is mentioned more than two hundred times in the Bible, it is never referred to symbolically. It is the setting of several major happenings in the Bible—the cleansing of Naaman from leprosy, the baptism of Jesus, the separation of its waters by Elijah and Elisha (twice), the floating of the axe head by Elisha, Gideon's victory over the Midianites, the separation of Lot from Abraham—but only one event has caused it to become a major symbol in spirituals and that is the crossing of the river by the Israelites on their way to the promised land. It is easy to understand why the story of Joshua leading the Israelites across the Jordan into the promised land would have an irresistible appeal to the slaves and their descendants. For the Israelites the crossing was the culmination of a long and arduous pilgrimage from bondage in Egypt to freedom in Canaan, an experience that would suggest obvious parallels to the lives of the slaves. In the process of adaptation in the spirituals, the river and the crossing itself became the basic symbols, and the other details of the story vanished—the careful preparation, the ceremonies during and after the crossing, the strategy for taking possession of the promised land. Stripped of all localizing restrictions, the symbol acquired the flexibility and independence needed to fulfill a variety of functions.

Most frequently the Jordan River symbolized the dividing line between this world and the next, between servitude and freedom. It was the final step on the long way to salvation, and crossing it represented the final victory. This meaning is expressed longingly and expectantly in "Deep River," in "Swing Low, Sweet Chariot," and in "I Couldn't Hear Nobody Pray." Sometimes the Jordan River becomes a symbol of difficulty in the struggle for a better life, as in "Stan' Still, Jordan," in "O, Wasn't Dat a Wide River?" and in "Oh the Winter Oh the Winter." In other songs the river symbolized not the difficulty of reaching the promised land but rather the promised land itself, as in "Roll, Jordan, Roll," in "I'm Goin' Down to the River Jordan," in "O Who Dat Comin?" and in "De Band of Gideon."

As the symbols were adapted to different usages in the spirituals, a sifting of the language took place with the result that some brief but powerful phrases survived to carry the symbols from one song to another. The phrases that symbolize the difficulty of achieving one's goals or dreams, for example, possess a simple eloquence that is seldom matched in other literature: "Jordan River is chilly an' cold (wide an' deep)" or "Jacob's ladder is deep an' long."

Conclusions about Symbols

Repetition, connotation, and allusion help us recognize and interpret symbols. In addition, we must develop a sensitivity to the felicitous use of language in general if we want to appreciate less obvious symbols. Any word or incident that calls attention to itself, anything unexpected, whatever seems particularly effective, should be looked at for symbolic implication. Some words and incidents seem incomplete until they are linked to others. Eudora Welty's "The Worn Path" is a powerful story if Phoenix Jackson's annual pilgrimage is taken literally, yet most of us would be unwilling to stop there. For one thing, our knowledge that any kind of journey in literature is nearly always symbolic makes us want to consider the possibilities in this story. If we work inductively through its episodes, we do indeed find symbolic implications that unify and enrich the story.

Although a symbol does not encourage the kind of comparison and interaction that we find in a metaphor, it can be as effective as a metaphor in enriching a literary work. For example, when Terence Rattigan in *The Browning Version* uses a timetable to present certain qualities in the central character, we don't merge the two or compare them, but we do accept the timetable as a concrete symbol for those traits. Throughout the play, Crocker-Harris prides himself on the precision with which he manages his professional and domestic life. He departs from this commitment briefly when he agrees to a change in the rules at the awards assembly; when he reverses himself at the end of the play, however, and decides that the usual rules must be followed after all, the timetable serves as an effective culminating symbol, reminding us of his sharp, cold intellect and devotion to protocol. The timetable symbolizes both the virtues and the flaws in the character of Crocker-Harris.

Many of our popular symbols appeal to us because of their concreteness and precision. Notice how much more interesting the following symbols are than their literal explanation in parentheses: We promise you a full dinner pail, a chicken in every pot, two cars in every garage (if we win the election, we promise to make you prosperous). The comic strip character Charlie Brown once consoled himself with a most effective symbol: the deuce of clubs. He counteracted his depression with the thought that sometimes even that lowly card takes a trick. A good symbol, like a good metaphor, produces pleasure; it can intensify, clarify, and expand literal language in many ways.

But that is not all. The fact that good symbols entice us to go from their literal meanings to their larger implications suggests that many symbols are miniature archetypes, that, in Platonic terms, they are particular manifestations of universal truths. We seem to be driven to find the greatest possible significance in everything we read and experience, to relate the small to the large, and to assure ourselves that ultimately everything is related and meaningful. This is a large subject that I want to discuss in greater detail in the next chapter.

Notes

1. Poetry textbooks and literary critics routinely discuss synecdoche and metonymy as examples of metaphor, which is a mistake. If the terms are to be discussed at all (I am not convinced that we really need them), they should be called symbols, for they merely ask the reader to make some rather obvious substitutions; they do not elicit comparisons. Tube for television set, threads for clothes, Oval Office for the White House, the pen for the press, the sword for the military, altar for church, red tape for bureaucracy, redneck for a bigot, blade for bulldozer—these are all synecdoches, a part standing for the whole. They are symbols that elicit varying degrees of connotation, but no comparisons. The same can be said about metonymy—using the name of one thing for something else closely related to it. There is nothing metaphorical about saying that you are reading Shakespeare when you are reading *Hamlet*. Now that some textbooks are using syndecdoche and metonymy interchangeably, both terms referring to one thing standing for another, there is all the more reason to avoid the words altogether and replace them with the term

symbol. Is anything gained, for example, by applying the term *metonymy* (or *synecdoche*) to the names of streets that have become well-established symbols for the things most closely associated with them: Wall Street and Park Avenue in New York, Fleet Street and Baker Street in London, Bourbon Street in New Orleans, Haight-Ashbury in San Francisco?

2. In this connection, the symbolism of titles might also be noted. Titles are conspicuous and often they provide a major symbol that is developed in the work. Among the story titles with symbolic import are Eudora Welty's "The Worn Path," H. H. Munro's "The Interlopers," Isaac Babel's "The Story of My Dovecot," Conrad Aiken's "Silent Snow, Secret Snow," Katherine Anne Porter's "The Jilting of Granny Weatherall," Shirley Jackson's "The Lottery," Anton Chekhov's "Gooseberries," and James Joyce's "Clay," "Araby," and "A Little Cloud." Novels with symbolic titles include Stephen Crane's *The Red Badge of Courage*, Joseph Conrad's *Heart of Darkness*, Ralph Ellison's *Invisible Man*, and Nathaniel Hawthorne's *The Scarlet Letter*.

6 The Ultimate Significance of Metaphor, Symbol, and Language

What we have already observed about the versatility of metaphor and symbol suggests that the creative potential of language is unlimited. When we recall the many ways in which we can use language and the many ways language can use us, we have reason to believe that language is not an inert tool but a dynamic force, that there must be a reciprocal relationship between language and life. To understand this relationship and its connection with metaphor and symbol, we need to examine three major miracles associated with language.

The first miracle concerns the manner in which a child learns language. Biolinguists now say that the way a child learns language has never been explained satisfactorily. Current theory suggests that a child has an inborn knowledge of the universal principles that control the operation and development of language. A child is not predisposed to learn any particular language but has the innate ability to learn all languages with equal ease. Children don't learn language; language grows in them. This is the first miracle—that a child is born with the capacity to learn any language and then is able to perfect whatever language he or she hears, even though that language is likely to be fragmentary and erratic, since parents do little in the way of formal language instruction. We come to the second miracle when we ask a simple question: How did a child ever acquire this amazing capacity for language?

Biolinguists agree that it was language that created us in the first place—literally created us and separated us from animals. Our development as human beings began when one of our remote ancestors discovered the advantage of using symbols of some kind that eventually developed into language. While animals continued to exist on the stimulus-response level, we rose to higher and higher levels as we learned to manipulate these newly acquired symbols. Language raised us "above the silence of plants and the grunts of beasts," or in Ibsen's metaphor, "Language was the hammer that caused inanimate matter to sing."[1] As Bertrand Russell observed, "No matter how eloquently a dog may bark, he cannot tell you that his parents were poor but honest."[2] As language grew, the brain grew to accommodate the need

for language. Even those who are not evolutionist agree that the onset
of language was instrumental in establishing our humanity.

When we look at the creation stories of various mythologies, we
find interesting examples of the interlocking of language with creation. Mythologies from all parts of the world contain accounts of
creation by language. In some of them the gods first create themselves
by giving themselves names, and they then use special words to create
the world. Several biblical passages also seem relevant to a consideration of the origin of language. According to Genesis, God created the
world by giving verbal commands and by giving names to four parts
of creation: day, night, heaven, and earth. The author of the book of
John echoes Genesis when he says: "In the beginning was the Word,
and the Word was with God, and the Word was God." It was this
passage that baffled Faust when he tried to usurp the revelations in
the New Testament by translating it into German. He doesn't get very
far, according to Goethe, but his efforts to alter it give him a glimpse
of the primordial significance of language and its interrelationship
with all aspects of life.

If we put together these two miracles based on the discoveries of
biolinguists, that we are born with the capacity to learn and perfect
language and that language literally created us, then we are prepared
to deal with the third and greatest miracle of all, the incredible power
of language either to accelerate the development of our humanity or
to destroy our humanity completely and return us to the level of
animals.

To understand this third miracle, we must remember that the
creative process associated with the first two miracles never stops.
When we use language we keep alive and advance the process of
creation, become co-creators with the vital forces that established and
developed our language and humanity. As George Steiner puts it
in *Extraterritorial: Papers on Literature and Language Revolution*
(Atheneum, 1971), "When mortals speak, they call into being whatever of the world is accessible to their senses and understanding.
The exercise of human language enacts, albeit on a microscopically
humble scale, the divine reflexes of creation, the Logos or 'speaking
into being' of the universe" (p. 75). This observation is closely related
to another recent conclusion of biolinguists.

The Constructive Power of Language

It is now pretty generally accepted that when we began using language
in the earliest stages of our development, we did so to satisfy a need

for self-expression rather than a need for communicating with others. We first used language to satisfy an inner compulsion, to relieve some kind of tension. That this is one of the creative functions of language that has never stopped can be verified by almost any number of testimonials.

The most vivid and the most frequently quoted example of the creative power of language is the experience of Helen Keller. Though blind and deaf after the age of two, she graduated with honors from Radcliffe and became a famous lecturer and author. In *The Story of My Life,* she describes how learning language opened new intellectual and emotional horizons:

> We walked down the path to the well-house. . . . Someone was drawing water and my teacher placed my hand under the spout. As the cool stream gushed over one hand she spelled into the other the word *water*, first slowly, then rapidly. I stood still, my whole attention fixed upon the motion of her fingers. Suddenly I felt a misty consciousness as of something forgotten—a thrill of returning thought; and somehow the mystery of language was revealed to me. I knew then that "w-a-t-e-r" meant the wonderful cool something that was flowing over my hand. That living word awakened my soul, gave it light, hope, joy, set it free! . . . I left the well-house eager to learn. Everything had a name, and each name gave birth to a new thought. As we returned to the house every object which I touched seemed to quiver with life.

Equally impressive are the statements of those who have experienced the therapeutic effect of writing. When Anne Frank shared her family's ordeal of hiding in very small rooms in Amsterdam to avoid detection by the Gestapo and almost certain death in a Nazi concentration camp, she wrote in her diary: "I can shake off everything if I write. My sorrows disappear, my courage is reborn . . . I can recapture everything when I write—my thoughts, my ideals, my fantasies."

Louis Simpson, a major contemporary poet, tells how writing helped him recover from the nervous breakdown he suffered after World War II:

> I got through the war all right, but afterward, when I was back in the States, I had a nervous breakdown and was hospitalized. I had amnesia; the war was blacked out in my mind; and so were episodes of my life before the war. When I left the hospital I found that I could hardly read or write. In these circumstances I began writing poems.
>
> Before the war I had written a few poems and some prose. Now I found that poetry was the only kind of writing in which I could express my thoughts. Through poems I could release the irrational, grotesque images I had accumulated during the war; and imposing order on these images enabled me to recover my identity.[3]

In *Soul on Ice,* Eldridge Cleaver tells of a similar experience: "When I returned to prison, I took a long look at myself and, for the first time in my life, admitted that I was wrong, that I had gone astray—astray not so much from white man's law as from being human, civilized . . . I lost my self-respect. My pride as a man dissolved and my whole fragile moral structure seemed to collapse, completely shattered. That is why I started to write. To save myself."

Helen Keller, Anne Frank, Louis Simpson, Eldridge Cleaver, and many others have experienced the humanizing effect of language because they respect its potential and use it creatively. Unfortunately, language can manifest its power in negative as well as in positive ways. It can actually contribute to the destruction of our humanity.

The Destructive Power of Language

The first step in the dehumanization process is apathy. When our growth in language reaches a plateau, when we lose interest in watching the way words are used, then language can hinder our growth as human beings. When we no longer recognize or deplore jargon and other abuses of language, we lay ourselves open to the greatest charlatans of all, those who use language to control us, deceive us, and dehumanize us. This is exactly what happens in the nightmare world of George Orwell's *1984.* The secret of Big Brother's domination of the actions, thoughts, and emotions of his subjects is his absolute control of their language. He replaces Oldspeak with Newspeak and decrees that love is hate, war is peace, freedom is slavery, ignorance is strength. But the slogans are only one of Big Brother's weapons. Just as important is the decimation of language, which occupies enormous teams of writers employed in the Ministry of Truth. The editor of the Eleventh Edition of Newspeak boasts that he has destroyed most of the old words and the ideas they represent. As he says to Winston, "Don't you see that the whole aim of Newspeak is to narrow the range of thought. In the end we shall make thoughtcrime literally impossible, because there will be no words in which to express it . . . every year fewer and fewer words, and the range of consciousness always a little smaller" (Part I, chapter 5). Big Brother knows that you shrivel minds when you shrivel language.

The apathy that makes possible atrocities like Newspeak is followed by atrophy and death. When we are mesmerized by language instead of refreshed by it, we have reversed the process of creation that was initiated by language. The very language that delivered us from the animal level is now allowed to brutalize us, both literally and figuratively. The logical outcome of this regression is the total loss of language, a situation that has been depicted all too vividly by various writers. For our first example of this catastrophe, we leave Orwell's world of unscrupulous politicians and enter Jonathan Swift's world of arrogant intellectuals.

In Book III of *Gulliver's Travels,* Swift devotes four chapters to depicting the life of theoretical scientists who are misusing their rational powers. We first meet them on the flying island of Laputa, where they are so far removed from the real world that they have lost their humanity. The most striking example of their inhumanity would seem to be that they are willing accomplices of the ruler of the island, who uses their discoveries to suppress and destroy disobedient subjects, but this is actually the result of a more basic dehumanization, namely, their destruction of their language. Their vocabulary and symbols are limited to mathematics and music, and they are hostile to everything else, having no words for ideas outside their own fields. They praise the beauty of a woman in terms of rhombs, circles, parallelograms, ellipses, and other mathematical terms, and their food is carved into the shapes of mathematical figures and musical instruments. They are unable to communicate unless a servant hits them on the ear with a small instrument called a flapper when they are supposed to listen, on the eyes when they are supposed to look up, and on the mouth when they are supposed to speak. They are detested by their wives, who are forced to seek companionship among servants and strangers. If they want to cheat on their husbands, they simply remove the servants with the flappers.

We now leave the flying island and follow Gulliver to Lagado, the largest metropolis in the kingdom, where some scientists who have spent five months on the flying island are allowed to advise the government and put their theories into practice. Even though their schemes have destroyed the countryside and deprived the people of food and clothing, they persist and have even formed an academy to continue their research. Here we find them trying to extract sunshine from cucumbers, convert ice into gunpowder, build houses from the top down, teach the blind to mix colors for painters, soften marble into pillows and pincushions, develop a solution that will prevent sheep from producing wool, and so on. All of these absurdities are but a prologue to the ultimate degradation we observe in the next two laboratories. First we see a professor and forty students operating a large frame with forty handles, ten on each side. Each handle is attached to a rod containing slips of paper with single words on them. As the rods are turned in various ways, words are brought to the surface. After each operation, the students eagerly survey the results to see whether by chance they have produced phrases that they might copy into their notebooks.

From this mechanization of our creative powers it is but a short step to the final laboratory where language is destroyed completely. Here the scientists who want to form a universal language have replaced words with things. Everyone carries a sackful of objects, and when people meet someone they want to talk to, they empty their sacks and point to the objects that replaced the words. Those who wish to conduct the most business carry the largest sacks. They walk down the streets doubled over into an animal posture, brutalized by the loss of language. The role of language in the creation of our humanity has been reversed.

Swift's point that the final and most important step in the destruction of our humanity is the destruction of our language is illustrated again and again in contemporary drama. When we read Ionesco, Pinter, Beckett, Albee, Pirandello, Osborne, and others, we soon discover that corruption of language is central to the corruption of life. Characters whose lives are empty talk nonsense, those confused about their aims in life talk past each other, those with deep-seated frustrations talk about peripheral trivialities to avoid facing their problems, those whose lives have been crushed make animal noises or become inarticulate. These plays demonstrate that language and personality are destroyed simultaneously. One is not the cause of the other because they are inseparable and, in a significant sense, identical.

Language and the Unity of Life

Let us now return to an examination of the positive potential of language. We have already seen the salutary effect of self-expression through language in the lives of Helen Keller, Louis Simpson, and others. We have yet to consider several other ways in which language contributes to our humanity.

Language developed in response to our need for self-expression, and it evolved as this primal urge blossomed into the insatiable curiosity that distinguishes our species. Language and our desire to know developed simultaneously and in a reciprocal manner. Our vocabularies expanded as we continued to interpret, label, and assimilate new facts and new experiences. Each new word became a symbol of yet another victory in our effort to transform confusion into clarity. We discovered that to understand something we have to be able to give it a name, and that when we name something we exercise some control over it. In Mary Shelley's novel, Victor Frankenstein did not give his monster a name, and he was unable to control it. One of the first assignments given to Adam in the Garden of Eden was to name all living creatures; he needed a set of verbal symbols to deal with his environment.

But language does more than provide us with labels; it also serves as the spark that keeps reigniting our curiosity and expanding our humanity. After Frankenstein's monster taught himself to speak, he attributed his earlier misery and cruelty to the fact that Frankenstein had not given him language. This reciprocal relationship between our language and our humanity may even be verifiable. Researchers are finding evidence that a growing vocabulary has a chemical effect on the brain, that it triggers new circuits, increases the versatility of the brain, and expands consciousness. There is even some evidence that using metaphors may have biological effects, igniting as Steiner puts it in *Extraterritorial*, "a new arc of perceptive energy" (pp. 67-68).

Language will continue to humanize us to the extent that we recognize it as a manifestation of the wholeness of life. Since the role of language in the development of our humanity is both intrinsic and continuous, it follows that our growing network of verbal symbols has never been broken and will never be broken, no matter how much it is expanded. This basic fact about language has been confirmed many times over by poets and others who work closely with words. As they develop a greater and greater sensitivity to language, these writers become aware of the ultimate unity of language as well as the ultimate unity of other aspects of life. They conclude that if our verbal symbols hang together, then the things they symbolize must also hang together. Lewis Thomas, distinguished scientist and author of *The Medusa and the Snail* and *The Lives of Cells,* says that becoming aware of the fact that all forms of life are somehow connected is one of the most impressive results of his research. John Donne observed in Meditation XVII that "no man is an island, entire of itself; every man is a piece of the continent . . . any man's death diminishes me, because I am involved in mankind; and therefore never send to know for whom the bell tolls; it tolls for thee." William Blake expressed the same conviction in "Auguries of Innocence":

> To see a World in a Grain of Sand
> And a Heaven in a Wild Flower,
> Hold Infinity in the palm of your hand
> And Eternity in an hour.

In "Flower in the Crannied Wall," Tennyson conveyed his vision of interrelatedness:

> Little flower—but *if* I could understand
> What you are, root and all, and all in all,
> I should know what God and man is.

It is this interrelationship of all things that makes it possible to express the abstract in the concrete, the universal in the particular, the many in the one, the macrocosm in the microcosm, the essence of many thoughts and feelings in the single metaphor or symbol.

This ultimate unity of all things is not just a vision of poets but a fact of life. Fractions are possible because we have whole numbers, analysis has its counterparts in synthesis, questions imply answers, causes have effects and effects have causes. Unity is implied in all our activities that involve dividing, combining, classifying, and organizing—taxonomies, typologies, paradigms, flow charts, computer programs, the Linnean categories in biology, school curricula, and on and on. The scientist assumes that each discovery can be differentiated from and then related to existing knowledge. When Albert Einstein died, Leonard Engel made the following observation ("What Einstein Was Up To," *Harpers*, December 1965):

> Although he may hardly be aware of it, modern man believes deeply in an orderly and coherent universe. He thinks that nature can be puzzling, but is not capricious; and that the cry of a bird is somehow related to the stately motions of the stars. If he did not think this, he could not be sure (as he is) that the sun will rise tomorrow; nor could he have confidence in his own power to manipulate the forces of nature.
>
> This idea of order and coherence in the universe is only an assumption. It can probably never be proved. The assumption would be greatly strengthened, however, if the universe could in fact be described as an orderly whole—in other words, if the diverse phenomena of nature could be brought under a single all-embracing law. It is just such a law Einstein sought.
>
> Curiously, Einstein stood nearly alone in the long search for a unified field theory. No doubt, this was due in part to the (as it turned out) appalling difficulty of the task. It stemmed also from the eager preference of most of his fellow physicists for keeping up with the rush of experiment; it is given to few to be deeply concerned with fundamentals (p. 69).

All our activities in the humanities are also based on the assumption of ultimate unity. Job's laments are so eloquent because they imply that life must be worth living, that God must be just. Lear also assumes an orderly universe when, holding the dead Cordelia in his arms, he asks, "Why should a dog, a horse, a rat, have life, and thou no breath at all?" Medieval and Renaissance writers used the circle as a symbol of unity and perfection. Eighteenth-century writers, with some help from Sir Isaac Newton, found nature to be controlled by a grand design that could be illustrated with an enormous chain, each link representing one segment of creation. Each generation, it seems, must develop its own unified field theory; if such a theory cannot be found, writers come forth with some variation of the Negro spiritual, "O I can't feel at home in this world any more." All these examples of unity go back to the unity in language, which is an extension of the basic unity that goes back to creation. Language is both the prototype and the agency of this unity.

Because of the interrelationship of all things, this unity in diversity, anything in the world can be compared to anything else. Not all comparisons succeed, of course, but some of our best metaphors, as we have seen, are daring comparisons. But a successful metaphor does more than merge seemingly incompatible terms; it demonstrates that the maker of the metaphor has developed both a keen sensitivity to language and a strong awareness of the unity of all things. As Aristotle said in chapter 22 of *On Poetics:* "But the greatest thing by far is to be master of metaphor. It is the only thing that cannot be learned from others; and it is also a sign of genius since a good metaphor implies an intuitive perception of the similarity in dissimilars."

Perhaps this discussion of the humanistic implications of metaphor can be concluded with an anecdote from the social sciences. An anthropologist once asked a tribal preacher why he used so many comparisons. The preacher replied that he used them to teach his people that the world is all one thing; he said that he used comparisons to defeat witchcraft since "witchcraft tries to break the world down and isolate men in order to eat them."[4] As C. Day Lewis put it in *The Poetic Image* (J. Cape, 1947), poets would seem to have the same aspirations as the tribal preacher: "There is a most remarkable weight and unanimity of evidence, both in the verse and the critical writings of English poets, that poetry's truth comes from the perception of a unity underlying and relating all phenomena, and that poetry's task is the perceptual discovery, through its imaging, metaphor-making faculty, of new relationships within this pattern, and the rediscovery and renovation of old ones" (p. 34).

Notes

1. Cited in George Steiner, *Language and Silence: Essays on Language, Literature, and the Inhuman* (Atheneum, 1967), 55.

2. Cited in Donna W. Cross, *Word Abuse: How the Words We Use, Use Us* (Coward, McCann & Geoghegan, 1979), 25.

3. Quoted in Ian Hamilton, *The Poetry of War* (Alan Ross, 1965), 171.

4. James W. Fernendez in *The Social Use of Metaphor: Essays on the Anthropology of Rhetoric,* ed. J. David Sapir and J. Christopher Crocker (University of Pennsylvania Press, 1977), 130.

Author

Roland Bartel teaches English at the University of Oregon, where he is also in charge of teacher certification in English. Past president of the Oregon Council of Teachers of English, Professor Bartel has published articles on the teaching of literature in *English Journal* and elsewhere. He is also an author-editor of *Biblical Images in Literature*.